C000110073

REMEMBERING ROMFORD

BRIAN EVANS

SUTTON PUBLISHING

Sutton Publishing Limited
Phoenix Mill · Thrupp · Stroud
Gloucestershire · GL5 2BU

First published 2005

Title page photograph: The Golden Lion corner, 1988. The attractive ancient inn and its neo-Georgian companion to the right (Lloyds Bank) are examples of buildings which add dignity to Romford. The Collectors Market in North Street echoes the human scale of its surroundings. Little can be said to commend the overbearing bulk of North House behind.

British Library Cataloguing in Publication Data
A catalogue record for this book is available from the British Library.

ISBN 0-7509-3856-0

Typeset in 10.5/13.5 Photina.
Typesetting and origination by
Sutton Publishing Limited.
Printed and bound in England by
J.H. Haynes & Co. Ltd, Sparkford.

This book is the main centennial project
of the Rotary Club of Romford (chartered 1922).
It commemorates 100 years of Rotary International,
which was founded in Chicago
on 23 February 1905 by Paul Harris.

Dedicated to the members of the Rotary Club of Romford
and its first lady president Susan Wolstenholme – 2004/5.

Funded with assistance from

Lottery Grants for Local Groups

AWARDS
FOR ALL

CONTENTS

Miss Harrington of 4 Albion Cottages, St Andrews Road, with her Blue Cross matches competition costume, hoping to win a prize in July 1930.

1

One Hundred Years of Moving Forward

In 1905 Romford was a quiet, tidy, respectable town. The peace was shattered chiefly on market days, at election junketings, and when the occasion arose to celebrate a royal anniversary or a coronation. At these times even the most respectable Rumfordian (as local folk were then known) might celebrate too well in the numerous public houses and inns with which the town was liberally supplied. On one occasion in the Market Place a member of the Poel family was only rescued at the last moment from the top of a huge bonfire at such a celebratory event. Luckily there had been a delay in lighting up. Dense crowds would make their appearance on the streets on such occasions within a very short time. To complement these 'feast' days, the town at other times could be as silent as the grave. The inhabitants would either be hard at work in their chosen occupations or taking part in their home in a form of family life that is not very common

Hardy-looking cattle tethered to the railings at the east end of the Market Place – a common sight here at the beginning of the twentieth century and up to the mid-1950s when the livestock market closed.

today. Nearly every home had a piano and impromptu entertainments at which each member of the family could perform in some way was then the norm.

A lot was due to change as the new century advanced, particularly in the last 50 years up to the millennium. In the early 1900s future marvels seemed a long way off. It was a gentler era with a different set of sounds and smells, hard for us to imagine today. The horse was still the universal mode of conveyance, and the clip-clop of hooves was one of the typical sounds. The noise of rumbling wagons was sometimes deadened by the placing of straw on the road outside a house where someone was ill or dying. Hospital treatment was a rare occurrence and home remedies and patent medicines in amazing quantities were the ordinary citizen's means of medical relief.

However, great advances in technology and medicine were on the horizon and in people's minds, as were struggles for equality such as that of the poor for better welfare and of women for a fairer deal, and the chance to vote for change. In the Edwardian era occasional glimpses of the first motor cars were being seen on Romford streets. The national press in the form of early popular newspapers, aimed at the masses who had only been included in elementary education for 30 years at the beginning of the century, gave a much-needed voice to the concerns of people at large. They were much valued as a source of information before the advent of cinema, radio and television. Importantly, local and national newspapers sometimes included predictions of life in the future. The novelist H.G. Wells, who also contributed to popular literature, was beginning to be a familiar celebrity known to many Romfordians. In *Land Ironclads* (1903) he had already described the tank and indicated that this weapon could be used in trench warfare. In 1906 his *War in the Air* forecast air warfare of the future, predicting that it would take place long before the year 2000, and perhaps before 1950. At the end of the First World War he predicted the atom bomb in his book *The World Set Free*. The bomb described by Wells could initiate atomic disintegration in a tiny fraction of bismuth. His most famous book *The War of the Worlds* caused a sensation when it was serialised on radio in America. Panic-stricken listeners believed the events described were actually taking place and jammed the switchboards of emergency services and the radio station. Wells and others also predicted more optimistic social and technical advances that would benefit mankind and make everyday life easier. Many of these improvements would be implemented by advances in the use and supply of power.

The Romford Gas Company, established in the nineteenth century, continued to produce and supply this means of providing cooking, lighting and increasingly, radiant heating to homes, and the latter to businesses. It was not until quite late in the century that the average home would be centrally heated and a boost to gas supply provided by finds of natural gas in the North Sea off the coast of Britain. Electricity, at first mainly for lighting, was introduced into Romford in 1915 by the County of London Electricity Supply Company, supplying power through the mains to a small area. A few mansions around the town, owned by the rich, installed small generators even earlier. For some years the new company took their power by agreement from private generators within Ind Coope's Romford Brewery. Quite soon they took over the brewery's generators, looking after them until 1924. At this date a separate substation was opened in Romford, and supplies now came from plant at the margarine manufacturers Jurgens, located at Purfleet to the south-east. The next year saw the opening of Barking Power Station, which enabled many more homes and businesses to be added to the system. Today we are used to a multiplicity of plug-in points in our homes, but houses built from the

Alice Cakebread seated on a new bike, a sister either side of her. A short ride away were the open fields and countryside. Cycling clubs were being formed everywhere in the early 1900s. Young people joined them to escape oppressive parental supervision.

1920s to the 1950s had very few. After this time it took many years for new wiring systems and multiple plugs to be installed to cope with the great number of new electrical appliances available in the domestic setting. There was tremendous rivalry in the 1920s and '30s between electricity and gas companies, and showrooms to promote the increased use of each type of power were opened in the town. The gas showroom in South Street was particularly well appointed with demonstration areas to show off all the latest appliances. Electricity gained ground as a means of lighting but many houses in the town remained gaslit through the '30s, '40s and '50s. Similarly, many houses remained without a general or central heating system until the 1960s, as gas central heating systems gradually gained popularity. Rumfordians sat in front of radiant gas or open coal fires while large portions of the house stayed cold. Electric blankets on beds and hot water-bottles made sleeping more comfortable.

The whole century can be seen to revolve around the use of various kinds of power. Further on we mention the dominance of the internal combustion engine in transport:

In the first half of the twentieth century coal reigned supreme as a fuel for household heating. A few built-in cooking ranges set into the kitchen wall have survived in Romford. Stoked by coal or other solid fuel they kept the kitchen and a small further part of the house warm in cold weather. Most houses stored the fuel either in a cellar or a coal store outside the house at the rear. Some solid fuel boilers heated more rooms in the house through large diameter hot-water pipes. In Romford there were several coal order offices in the station yard, where the bus station now stands.

in spite of all the refinements it is still basically unchanged in design from the earliest examples of automobiles seen on Romford streets. Some of the early motor cars used alternative systems involving steam and electricity. In some ways the industry has failed so far to develop a less polluting vehicle. In Romford electricity has been developed in many other ways: the two early cinemas provided entertainment powered by this source from just before the First World War. The gramophone began to harness electrical recording of music and voice and was sold to the Romford public from about the same time. The local council, on 6 October 1913, received a letter from Mr S. Warburton seeking permission to play a gramophone on his stall on market days. Councillor Dowsing proposed and Councillor Rich seconded a resolution that the instrument 'is played only at the request of an intended purchaser to demonstrate its capabilities etc., and that the Market Collector have power to withdraw such permission if he deems if advisable'. Today we have the ultimate successor to the gramophone, which used a fixed needle to generate music and speech from a revolving disc horizontally placed on the machine . . . it is known as the iPod!

Electricity came to railways elsewhere in selected parts of Britain. The Southern Railway and the Mersey Railway were electrified by the 1920s but the London & North Eastern Railway through Romford retained the use of steam engines until after the Second World War. No doubt the two wars held up many potential developments locally as elsewhere in Britain. An attempt was made to introduce electric street tramways into the town at the beginning of the twentieth century but all the plans foundered because of the much narrower High Street and South Street roadways of the time and vociferous local opposition. The London General Company's motor bus service from inner London to Gidea Park just before the First World War provided a flexibility for local travel denied to the railway service. Across South Street's railway bridge up to 1930 there was only a single-track service each way up and down to London. This encouraged a tremendous growth in bus services and the town is still reasonably served up to the present day. The bridge was reconstructed in 1930 and the whole line widened across a bigger embankment, allowing fast trains to bypass stopping services.

Before this in the mid-1920s a huge scheme to provide employment for ex-servicemen involved the building of a wide arterial road around the northern and eastern margin of central Romford and Gidea Park. This we now know as Eastern Avenue and the scheme in its entirety created a new fast link from the North Circular Road in the west all the way to Southend in the east. Although only a minority of the population owned a car, the internal combustion engine was beginning to make an impression on the landscape, and to eat into the countryside and farmland. Because of economic recession, the road was for many years underused.

Perhaps for the same reason living conditions in the town changed only slowly for most people in the 1920s, though more and more rapidly in the succeeding decades of the century. Educational standards rose and there were new opportunities for the educated person, and to a certain extent for new businesses. The rise in modern electrical power comes into play here. The story of one business in Romford can be used to sum up how things changed. We have mentioned the beginning of electrical entertainment on Romford Market. A very significant date for the century was the opening of national radio broadcasting: the BBC was formed in 1922 – the same year as Romford Rotary Club. The local business known as Silcocks had been founded in Romford High Street in 1860, when it traded under the heading of 'plumbers, painters, glaziers and house decorators'. Eric, the eldest son, became interested in wireless (as radio broadcasting was then known), in the first instance as a hobby after the First World War. It was still a revolutionary new discovery. He managed to persuade his father Harold and a close friend, Frank Hardingham, to invest £3 each for the purchase of crystal set parts (crystal detectors, slider tuning coils, terminals and so forth) to be displayed in the shop. Crystal sets were the first available radio receivers, involving much tinkering with the crystal, or cat's whisker, to tune into a programme. Public interest soon grew. The High Street premises became more devoted to the radio business, and were enlarged, taking over the next-door shop, vacated by the Kistlers. Wireless sets were soon run from a 2, 4 or 6-volt current, derived from a cumbersome battery device, known as an accumulator, which lit up large glass valves inside the set. Such accumulators had to be re-charged at least once a week. The new Silcocks business eventually constructed charging equipment run from the brewery's private generating station. They were thus able to collect or receive accumulators brought to them by the public on their premises, as well as selling new wireless sets. The growth in Romford homes possessing what became known as radio facilities led to Romfordians becoming informed through news broadcasts about events around the world.

A 1935 advertisement shows a typical kitchen scene of the time.

Local people were also developing a weekly or twice-weekly cinema-going habit and programmes began to include a newsreel from Pathé, Gaumont-British and other news-gathering agencies. Television was only just beginning to appear in the wealthier homes in the 1930s. There was no comprehensive television news. Of course many Romfordians listened to the radio and went to the cinema for the music and entertainment to liven up what were then rather drab daily lives and homes.

Returning to the Silcocks' business, the company purchased a van, later to become a fleet, and the vans were painted bright yellow! At a time when most vehicles were black this was a masterstroke of advertising and led to the firm's name being noticed all over Romford. Silcocks were the first to think up an idea that got them noticed, and it led to quite a few Romford businesses developing similar techniques, such as bold lettering or striking shopfronts. As the 1920s advanced into the 1930s Romford's South Street was becoming a business hotspot and locals started to call it the Golden Mile. Silcocks opened a smart new shop in this important location following an offer by Tommy England, who owned properties all over the town. A photograph of 1936 shows the large plate-glass windows with radios prominently displayed inside and a small number of the newest thing – the amazing television, but this luxury was too expensive for most local families. At this time the large TV console housed only a tiny screen. The BBC producers were putting out programmes for just a few hours a day and the clarity of the picture was questionable. It was easier to visit the new super cinemas and sit in luxurious comfort

Left: The 1934 Gidea Park Modern Homes Exhibition catalogue had this advertisement for an electric washing machine. Only the wealthier inhabitants could afford such luxury. It would be many years before the majority of Romfordians owned the 1960s version on hire purchase. *Right:* The case for electricity in the 1930s.

These small businesses on the bend of London Road gave a touch of Victorian character to the section east of the Sun public house, seen in about 1990. They have been replaced by an extension to a car showroom.

compared with most home conditions for a relatively small entrance fee. The old Laurie 'flea-pit' cinema at the end of the market and the Victory, towards the top end of South Street, were overshadowed in the 1930s by the Havana (later the Odeon), the Plaza (later the Gaumont), and finally the Ritz, opened in 1938, later the ABC and the Cannon. Cinema going had become the major entertainment in most people's lives. These electronic wonders were to be a great source of keeping up morale when war broke out in 1939. For a short time when hostilities were declared the Government ordered them to be closed but soon realised its mistake. Playing their part in keeping the nation's chin up they screened a succession of patriotic films about wartime; strangely one of the most important was the historical picture *Henry V* with its stirring scenes of preparation for battle. Silcocks' small South Street shop was actually destroyed by an enemy landmine during an air raid in 1940. In any case war had already brought a halt to the

A view over the rooftops at the south-west end of the Market Place reveals open fields and tree-lined slopes towards the north.

Opposite: Towards the end of the twentieth century this striking shopfront overlooked the south-west end of the Market Place. It illustrates a remarkable saga of continuity. The shop stands on the site of the former Macarthys chemist's shop founded in 1787 at a time when prosperity was brought to Romford by the coaching routes through the town between London and East Anglia. Up to the 1960s/'70s the sign still proclaimed it as Liberty Chemists. Since then ownership has changed several times, but it is still trading as a chemist at the time of writing. The old-fashioned gable and top floor window remain from a re-creation of the original shopfront of 1787, which was reconstructed by Macarthys in 1935. Modern trading needs unfortunately dictated the removal of the quaint lower floor window fitted up in eighteenth-century style and the substitution of the current 'open' entrance.

tremendous expansion just before the war, and a Dagenham branch of the business had to be closed at the outbreak. Trading conditions became very difficult. The technical staff, with their knowledge of radio, were particularly in demand to join the RAF. Eric Silcock was by chance never called up. He carried on with the business, employing many women to fill the gaps vacated by the men in the accumulator workshops, the only section to keep going throughout the war years. The government of course encouraged the population to keep their radios maintained at a time when they needed to communicate wartime information to the general public. Apart from the good advice about making the most of the food ration by ingenious recipes, it was always possible that immediate announcements might need to be made in the event of a German invasion. The women played a vital part in all this – the work of charging assistants for the accumulators was not an attractive job. Accumulators were filled with acid and small splashes would ruin clothes, at a time when new ones were almost impossible to buy and rationed by a coupon system.

By 1945 a new site had had to be found in Mildmay Road for the accumulator-charging operation which had continued throughout the six long years of war. The days of the old High Street were already numbered in 1939, because plans for the demolition of old properties and the widening of the roadway were coming to a head. New retail premises were leased in North Street where the pedestrianised section is today. Televisions were now becoming more popular, with larger screens and more hours of broadcasting. It was the coronation of Queen Elizabeth II in 1953 that began the stampede and showed what the medium could do to entertain. Gradually more and more homes acquired a set, and radio was also booming, with children's and adults' programmes being listened to avidly by all the family. The wartime habit of switching on for the news had encouraged this.

This was a boom period, but there were clouds on the horizon, for Silcocks as for other local businesses. Several factors began to eat into the prosperity. Growing red tape, various new taxes and greater traffic congestion meant that the firm's yellow service vans were able to visit fewer homes in the day as time went on. Eventually, in the early 1960s an attempt was made to sell the business but this proved difficult, in spite of the famous Macmillan government slogan 'You've never had it so good'. At this time quite a number of local businesses in Romford were struggling. It seemed that it was to be an era of the national businesses with their chains of branches to take over – they were able to cope more efficiently at the central point with the new demands of regulation and paperwork before smaller computers became available everywhere.

2

The Long Edwardian Summer

In 1905 walking was a necessity in Romford since there were no buses or trams. As Edward Fisk wrote, 'You walk to church, to post a letter, or to buy anything'. The roads 'were bad, narrow, even the High Street. They were made with gravel or grit, hardened by steam roller. Some were not paved, but the Market Square was cobbled.' South Street was taking over gradually from businesses in the High Street and Market Place as a main shopping centre. Shops gradually spread down the Golden Lion corner as the line of private houses along the street began to be replaced by business premises. This was spurred on by the movement down the street to a new premises by the Post Office, again just before the First World War. On the western side below the Western Road junction there were still private houses; opposite were more houses and the County Court and nearer the station a new terrace of shops with office premises above down to the corner of Eastern Road. This is now of course the location of the bar and restaurant area which I call Costa del South Street, as the outdoor seating reminds people of continental holidays.

Edward Fisk remembered, 'The brewery delivered beer by horse and cart in all directions to the country around, and by way of rural lanes to outlying villages. Shops were mostly dingy and badly lit due to the fire risk of internal gas lighting, all that was available. All purchases were wrapped up in brown paper and tied with string.' Very few shop products came packaged in colourful pre-wrapped boxes and tins at the beginning of the century. Fisk also remembered the state of housing in the early twentieth century: 'mostly terraced, or three or four together in blocks, with four-room accommodation and small wood framed, often sash windows. Few working-class houses (the majority) had bay windows. Front doors were of wood, with iron knockers on the outside instead of bells. These houses were normally rented at 3s. 6d. to 5s. per week from a local landlord whose family had built them. Surprisingly, many of the poorer houses had a sizeable garden compared with many contemporary houses. These houses were heated by coal fires with one fitted oven or range of iron inserted in the wall. Open fires had to be guarded by wire fenders, fireguards, fire irons and shovels were used to manipulate the wood and coal in the grate. There was usually a shed and a dog kennel in the garden, also a mangle to squeeze water out of newly washed clothes and bed linen, together with a chopping block to break up logs for the fire. A dark and primitive wash-house contained a copper for the laundering of clothes, usually heated by a coal fire underneath.

Working-class houses always had an outside toilet and a cold water tap outside which was often shared between two families'.

At that time the majority of people were seeking respectability in everyday life. It was important that others thought well of them. This was not always easy to achieve. There was a pyramid of a class system, ranging from the near aristocracy, comfortably ensconced in their big houses in Havering village and on the outskirts of the town, down to the lowest sections of the out of work, desperately trying to survive in primitive conditions. It would be a few years yet before a Liberal government introduced a basic social security system. In 1905 probably 85 per cent of the local population might drift into poverty through the accident of illness, business failure, farming or business lay-offs of workers. Then the prospect of the workhouse threatened, where you were at the mercy of officials. A few people who experienced it remembered with gratitude the help given by this institution, but to most it was a dreadful place of discomfort and of course a place where you lost your self-respect.

From the working class up to the lower middle class, even office staff and younger professionals all rented their homes, usually from a local builder or estate agent, and rents were mostly collected weekly. Edward Fisk remembered the typical furnishing of a steadily employed worker's home: a three-piece suite in the front room, wooden chairs in the living room. In the bedroom iron bedsteads with flock mattress, and feather bed for the parents. A built-in wardrobe, chest of drawers and a dressing table completed the bedroom. The houses and rooms being fairly small, the stairs were often quite steep to fit in to the available space. The floors of all the rooms were lino covered, with a few mats laid here and there. Walls were papered or whitewashed. Pianos were not often seen in the town, but always a lot of china or glass ornaments, many of these being arranged on the mantelpiece in the main sitting room, a kind of treasure trove of the family's past history.

Fisk also reported that lighting would be by oil lamp, and the family went to bed by candlelight. All wore nightdresses, mostly of flannel. Boys and girls in big families would sleep in the same bed, sometimes head to toe. Knives and forks were made of steel, and had to be polished with brick-dust. Tea-sets and dishes were all of earthenware rather than china. Meat was kept in a zinc-doored safe in the wash-house or other cool place. No refrigerators then, nor any running hot water in the house.

'Generally people wore three-piece suits for the men – long dresses for the ladies. All wore boots and not shoes, and hats. The men a cap or bowler hat, the ladies large flowered hats. Women were tightly corseted and were prone to fainting. Men had watch chains across their middle, with a watch and key on either side. Men's shirts were stiffened and had no collars. Separate collars were very stiff and fastened to the shirt neck by collar studs, ties the same way. Boots were all leather, button-up or lace-up. Overcoats were heavy and there were no macs. A walking-stick was an essential for the man, having a bone handle, and, of course, an umbrella. Men used braces to hold up their trousers, everything was button-up and no belts were needed.

'Moving on to activities, we have mentioned that walking was a necessity. For leisure in Romford, cricket was *the* game, and football next in popularity. Tennis was for ladies, with underarm service – there were many tennis courts dotted about on the frequent vacant spaces in the town. Romford was not then all built up. Ping-pong was played by many. It could be played on the large dining-room tables then installed in many houses.

At home one played ludo or snakes and ladders, perhaps draughts, but not chess. We played billiards, not snooker. There was a lot of drunkenness, beer being so cheap. It was part of your fun to see drunks hauled to the police station in South Street on Saturdays.

'There was no Town Hall and no Public Library. No theatre, music hall or cinema existed in the town. Except for a temporary entertainment hall, for a short time at the bottom of Victoria Road. We walked to Ilford Hippodrome and back to see the music hall there. Although there was no orchestra, the Town Band was in Raphael Park on Sundays, and there were other bands. In the winter skating was allowed on the lake. Churches and chapels were well attended. Everyone went to church on Sunday evening in their best suits and dresses. There were Boy Scouts and Church Lads' Brigades, and also the Boys' Brigade for the younger element. With Britain very jingoistic the Territorial Army, earlier known as the Volunteers, was an occupation for the older lads.

'We were taught the three Rs thoroughly, but no further education after fourteen years. No exams, only a blue certificate that one had gone to school. Slates were used, therefore saving the cost of paper. The cane was given for any serious offence. Surviving childhood illnesses was quite an achievement. One paid for doctor's visits, so we joined the Hospital Saving Association, or similar medical benefit clubs. Tuberculosis was the killer disease, many a child was taken away to an isolation hospital never to be seen again. Perhaps families were large, partly to compensate for the number of childhood deaths, but also of course, there was no effective birth control. Vaccination against smallpox was semi-compulsory. Rickets in children was common, causing bow legs. Many proprietary medicines were widely advertised and used, such as Beecham's pills. Common remedies were cod-liver oil and brimstone and treacle. Men worked up to ten hours a day. Wages were £1 to £2 per week. Generally only men smoked. Offices were poorly lit, and the desks were long, clerks being perched on high stools with no backs.'

It should be remembered how unbuilt up Romford was before the First World War and even some time afterwards. Both the centre and surrounding areas contained much open space in the form of front gardens, vacant lots, allotments and market gardens. The building line in North Street above the Golden Lion petered out after Como Street and Park Villas opposite. Mrs D.H. Starr remembered the high wall below the trees on the right-hand side which encircled the Marshalls Estate – 'a lovely park which stretched from North Street around Havering Road, right round to Pettits Lane, which latter was a beautiful country lane, one of the favourite walks for Romfordians. Havering Road (leading up to Mashiters Hill) was an avenue of trees, which met, making a canopy over one's head. The only house in that lane was the large house called Priests. Gone are the days when one could walk down Collier Row Lane in the dusk and hear the call of the fox. Occasionally one of these would leap over the hedge in front of you and dash across the road. In those days there was the Bell Inn and not more than half a dozen cottages in the lane.'

In a house named Southfields in Havering Road lived George Hobday, who cultivated a new variety that became known as 'Hobday's Giant Rhubarb'. This was sold through Cutbush's nursery at Highgate, and became widely known for its excellent flavour and strong roots. Horticulture was one very important element of the local economy. The Hobday family business was an estate agency in Romford, another significant activity in the district, which of course led to the amazing growth of the town from this time on.

A classic scene looking down South Street, *c.* 1905. The left-hand side shows the range of buildings which were compulsorily purchased by Romford Council and demolished in the 1930s to widen the roadway and pavement. These include the Fox & Hounds, one of Romford's lost hostelries, once the meeting place of the town's clubs and societies in Victorian and Edwardian times. On the right-hand corner is the famous chemist's business of Lashams, founded in the nineteenth century and taken over in the early twentieth by the businessman and entrepreneur Tommy England. The tall building in the middle on the right-hand side was the post office which had continually moved about over the decades, starting in the Market Place and later in the High Street when this was the main commercial centre. The shops in South Street were increasingly being added to, superseding the private houses until they reached down to the station bridge. There was a big expansion in shopping facilities at this time, amounting to an Edwardian commercial boom.

A market day display in early twentieth-century Romford, showing a wide range of the agricultural equipment available to visiting farmers. The famous Hornchurch firm of Wedlake which produced many new versions of ploughs, rakes, seed drills and so on for a long time had a depot at the top of South Street to cater for this demand. Long centuries of tradition that made Romford's market days of great importance to the farming community stretching a long way out into Essex and allowing the week's agricultural business to be transacted, lived on. But consumer and professional interests that had played a smaller part were soon to loom much larger in significance when a commercial and residential boom overtook the agricultural interest, putting Romford on the map in quite a different way. The first motor bus service to the town was soon to be operated by the London General Omnibus Company, connecting the town with the rest of London and bringing tourists on day trips to gawp at Romford's eccentric mix of town and country life and people.

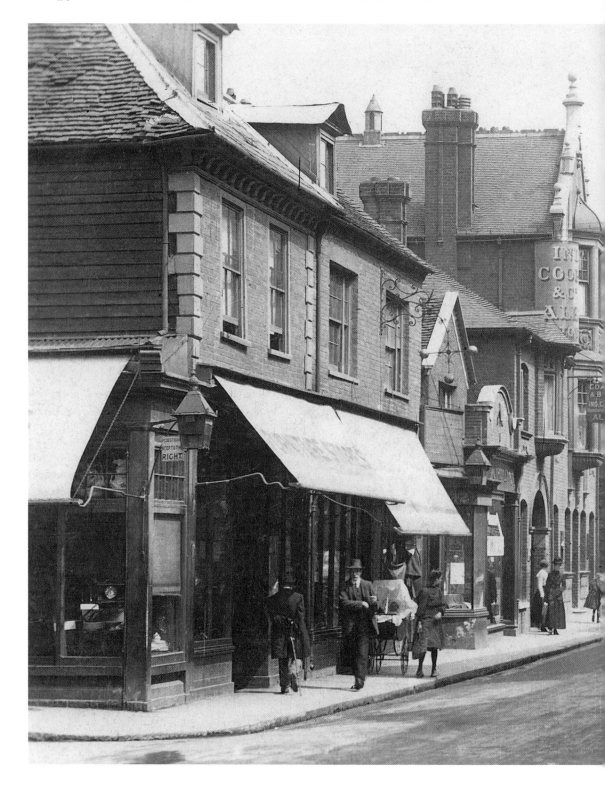

Previous pages: Old High Street, Romford, had once been the principal shopping area in the town, apart from the Market Place, and there were still a considerable number of local businesses cheek by jowl as can be seen. Behind the photographer the street continued almost unbroken in a shallow curve, joining up with London Road as it passed Waterloo Road. In the middle of the picture the tallest building is the Coach & Bell Public House, which had been rebuilt to replace a more ancient timber structure. South Street round the corner was gradually filling up with shops, and by the 1930s would be Romford's most important group of retail businesses.

Left: An elegant neo-Georgian doorway in the High Street. This 1930s rebuild shames some of the shoddy new construction of recent years which detracts from Romford's real character.

From a viewpoint opposite Waterloo Road on the right, the western end of the High Street is visible with its collection of premises dating from many centuries and its multitude of small businesses. Cakebreads, the largest store in the street, sold 'good bread, flour and confectionery' and was known as the West Grocery Stores.

Above: Pictured by the very busy local photographer E.E. Carter, of the Cottages Studios, Romford, this local football team have notably managed to acquire a set of shirts almost all of the same pattern. In the Edwardian golden age the sport was followed by many amateur teams with almost as much passion as the professional teams of more recent times.

Left and opposite: Sir Herbert Henry Raphael, originator of the Gidea Park Garden Suburb, the idea for which stemmed from his purchase of the old Gidea Hall Estate. Starting with the founding of a golf club on the eastern portion, Raphael donated some of the land at the western end as a park for the use of the townspeople – Romford's first. He changed the local landscape even further by creating a new suburb in the middle portion of the estate around the old hall, setting up a scheme to erect cottages and small houses of excellent design. The scheme developed in the form of an exhibition with some of the best architects of the time vying to produce model houses within a budget and with prizes for those adjudged the winners. These are early views of newly built houses and cottages, top in Parkway and below in Elm Walk. Today the Gidea Park Civic Society works hard to retain the Arts and Crafts character of this special enclave.

An early view of Reed Pond Walk shows some of the
distinctive designs of the houses which formed part of
the original exhibition, before a shrubbery grew up on
the central open space. The pond reminds us that there
were problems with water levels on the new estate in the
early days, which led for instance to the draining of the
Spoon Pond in Raphael Park.

In the early twentieth century the post office stood in the middle of the left-hand side of the then extremely narrow top end of South Street. On the left were some ancient dwellings which had been converted into shops before the era of strict planning regulations. The interiors were very dark owing to the difficulty of illuminating them without fire risk, in days of primitive oil and gas lamps.

Main Road was beginning to acquire some large houses built for the more well to do business and professional people attracted to the growing town. Nearly all the frontages on to the street were well guarded by strong walls and fences. Dr Harold Upward lived in more than one of these houses in succession. Latterly his house and surgery was on the corner of Junction Road and though the house has now been demolished, Upward Court, a group of flats, now occupies the site. The solid houses in the picture may well have been the earliest to use electricity for lighting, and still exist, though they are not usually now occupied as private houses.

Western Road, laid out as one of Romford's smartest Victorian and Edwardian streets, housed many of the town's more important citizens. It epitomises Romford's original very compact centre, where most facilities were close at hand. Here the long unbroken avenue can be seen but with some open spaces between the houses. Further up on the left hand side was a linear nursery (what would now be known as a garden centre) running through to the Market Place near the Laurie Hall and Laurie Square. Through this until the middle of the twentieth century ran a quiet and pleasant pathway – a privilege path open to the public except for one day in the year so that the nursery's owner could assert his legal rights to ownership.

A 1960s view of the Midland (now HSBC) Bank building at the north-west end of the Market Place, which in 1905 replaced some rather ancient structures used as shops. Such new Edwardian construction emphasised the growing financial and professional clout being exercised by Romford.

At the same time as Romford was acquiring a more up-to-date rather than a provincial character, the old-established market continued to function much as it had done for centuries, and it was the very fact that farmers and buyers had to come to Romford in great numbers that enabled the town to grow in commercial prosperity in other ways. The twentieth century demanded a new outlook, a new professionalism and the introduction of outside finance. Superficially, the great changes that were to come were for a number of years developing unnoticed as the auctioneers and cattle dealers pursued their regular market dealings. Romford was to retain much of its historic fabric into the 1920s before local business deemed much of it old fashioned and out of date, not realising that this encapsulated some of Romford's attraction.

An Edwardian idyll. Dora Collier enjoys the freedom of unrestricted play in the extensive garden of her parents' house in Junction Road by the stream (Black's Brook) which later feeds by underground ways into the Rom. At the back of the property running across to Squirrels Heath and Balgores Lane were the open spaces of Payne's Fields, a favourite walk for Romfordians, now partly covered by Carlton and adjoining roads.

3

European Conflict

Afternoon the assassination of Archduke Ferdinand at Sarajevo patriotic fervour swept the streets of Romford. One Romfordian was actually working in Germany when war broke out and had some rather curious experiences in his efforts to join up on returning to England. John Hewitt had left the engineering office 'full of Germans who were dumbfounded at the temerity of England in daring to challenge the greatest military power in history', in 1914. Arriving in England, in spite of all the patriotic propaganda calling on men to enlist in the army or navy, Hewitt found it was not as simple to do so as he would have expected. In Hewitt's words, 'The navy seemed not to want you', so he then tried the rounds of army recruiting departments: 'The Westminster Rifles took my name and address and thought that they might be able to let me know soon. The London Scottish did the same. I tried the "Roughriders". No luck. Thousands of teenagers and older men were already in these and similar territorial units and had been for years, but the War Office was apparently quite unprepared to deal with the 1914 surge of recruits, from what had been styled previously "England's effeminate youth". However, I had stupidly overlooked the opportunities on my own doorstep. My cousin, also a Romfordian and aged 17, had beaten me to it. He had already joined the Romford Territorial Battery of Field Artillery, giving his age as 18 – the minimum. The unit's HQ were just a little way up Hornchurch Road (now South Street), on the right. "Come and join there", he said. "They are mostly local chaps. We already know some of them. You'll have to see Dr Fraser's dispenser to have your eyesight tested. Go down there without your glasses and look through your fingers; you'll probably get away with it." I did get away with it, so on 3 October 1914 I became a gunner and took the oath. Then still in civilian clothes we began foot drill. On the left of Hornchurch Road (South Street) after passing Victoria Road corner, where the shops are now, and roads behind, there was in those days an open field. It was here that we went through our first movements drilled by a corporal.'

In contrast to the experiences of John Hewitt an army unit of people mostly from outside the town moved to Romford to occupy the fields and meadows of the Hare Hall estate. With an entrance on Main Road, a whole hamlet of wooden army huts were constructed, serviced by drainage and electricity through the expertise of members of the unit. This was the Artists' Rifles – from being a volunteer regiment like many of those being formed it soon became an Officer Training group. Sir John French had recognised the excellent pool of experience and knowledge available in the Artists' Rifles and set them up in this role. The site of most of this camp is now occupied by Castellan Avenue, Wallenger Avenue and adjoining roads. The camp at the time contained many facilities that made it practically self-sufficient. The Artists' Rifles had such prestige that officer cadets joining actually had to pay a fee for the privilege at the Dukes Road, St Pancras, HQ in London.

An impeccably turned-out soldier with fixed bayonet stands outside the guard hut at the entrance to Hare Hall camp. A clipboard with the Orders of the Day can be seen propped up inside the hut.

Photographed by his father, the son of Romford photographer E.E. Carter poses with his friends in the garden at the back of the studio.

A First World War view of the Golden Lion corner. The policeman at the corner whose duty was to control traffic movements looks like PC Cook, who appears in many photographs taken at this time. The soldier may be from any one of the Regiments mainly billeted in schools all round the town. For instance the first Herts regiment at a later stage left a message on the blackboard of Mawney Road School in the form of a poem called 'The Gun Team Song', the first verse of which ran as follows:

> Onward boys of the gun team
> Marching to the Rhine
> With their guns and tripods
> Coming on behind
> Captain Boyd our leader
> Leads against the foe
> Forward into battle
> See the gun team go.

Behind these figures the day-to-day life of civil Romford carries on, highlighted by the back view of a quaint horse-carriage proceeding up South Street, where a sign behind the Golden Lion advertises a Temperance Hotel.

Your King and Country need you.

A CALL TO ARMS

AN addition of **100,000** men to His Majesty's Regular Army is immediately necessary in the present grave National Emergency.

Lord Kitchener is confident that this appeal will be at once responded to by all those who have the safety of our Empire at heart.

TERMS OF SERVICE.

General Service for a period of 3 years or until the war is concluded.   Age of enlistment between 19 and 30.

HOW TO JOIN.

Full information can be obtained at any Post Office in the Kingdom or at any Military Depot.

God Save the King.

This is the rewrite of the enlistment advert by Lord Kitchener on 11 August 1914, which was to be published in newspapers and magazines.

A second picture of E.E. Carter's son and his group reveals that while they have all joined up he will have to stay at home in civilian life because of a disability.

A view of the magnificent huts and duckboard paths put up by the Artists' Rifles to house the Second Battalion in the grounds of Hare Hall. Some of the principal officers were actually billeted in the Hall itself and in Balgores at the top of Balgores Lane, later used as a school.

A large hut contained this reading room, organised by the Young Men's Christian Association (YMCA), who played a significant part in the welfare of soldiers during the First World War. The attitude of the men present does indicate a more confident and educated origin than the typical 'Tommy' of 1914–19. Not a few of the men in the Artists' Rifles were well above the average age of recruits.

The YMCA was also very active in the battlefield areas of France and Belgium.

Above: A group of soldiers get down to work digging trenches in the Romford area as part of their training for combat in France, *c.* 1916.

Left: A smiling group from the Artists' Rifles wearing the distinctive puttees typical of First World War troops pose for the photographer against the peaceful tree-lined vistas of Gidea Park in 1918.

Before the Tanks had Cleared the Village.

Mr. PERCIVAL PHILLIPS, in his despatch, writes:—

The familiar and ever-welcome sign of the Y.M.C.A. blossomed on a roofless French café, six miles within the crumpled German line; before the tanks had finished chasing the Staff of the Eleventh Corps out of Framerville and down the Peronne road. Food and even books and papers were set out under the Red Triangle for the tired and hungry fighting men, and they trooped into the rickety building to eat and be refreshed in a room carpeted with German papers.

Mr. W. BEACH THOMAS, in his despatch, "With the British," writes:—

Not far from them was a German notice board. I hear from an officer who visited the spot again a day later that another notice, "This way to the Y.M.C.A.," was added.

A dashing cavalry officer, very much of the old school, possessing a voice that would carry about two miles, begged me with great earnestness to do him one service. Would I mention the Y.M.C.A.? It had provided his men with hot coffee before riding out.

Donations should be addressed to Sir HENRY E. E. PROCTER, Acting Hon. Treasurer, Y.M.C.A. National Headquarters, 13, Russell Square, London, W.C. 1. Cheques should be made payable to Sir Henry E. E. Procter, and crossed Barclay's Bank, Ltd.

BEFORE the Tanks had finished chasing the German Staff out of Framerville—so runs the War Correspondent's message—the Y.M.C.A. were serving our tired and hungry soldiers with breakfast in a roofless French café. Our men are fighting in a country nearly bare of shelter, where the Germans have burned and destroyed everything possible. That is why the Y.M.C.A. is rushing forward mobile outfits, in which our men can find shelter, rest and refreshment. The demand for this rapid extension of our work has come suddenly. It places a heavy additional strain upon our resources, and we most earnestly appeal to you to help by sending a gift of money, as liberal as you can make it.

Help to meet the urgent needs of our Victorious Soldiers

You can give that help without leaving your home or your office, by sending a cheque to the Y.M.C.A. to-day. Do not leave it to others—see to it yourself.

Our workers in France have sent an urgent appeal for at least 150 mobile outfits, consisting of a marquee, furniture and canteen to enable them to follow each stage of the advance. The cost of these outfits is **£375** each, smaller size **£245. Will you give one complete**, to be named as you desire?

Please send all you can afford.

If you can contribute a cheque for £1,000, post it to-day, and be glad that you can do so much for our splendid fighting men. If you can only afford a shilling do not hold back. At least one soldier will have cause to bless you.

Will you post this to-day?

To Sir HENRY E. E. PROCTER, Y.M.C.A. National Headquarters, 13, Russell Sq., London, W.C. 1.

I have pleasure in enclosing £.......................... towards the special work of the Y.M.C.A. for the Troops.

Name...

Address...

Punch Almanack..

Registered under the War Charities Act, 1916.

Opposite, above: An appeal for funds in the *Punch Almanac* for 1919 shows how the YMCA effectively supported battle-weary troops in the front line in France.

Left and above: Oldchurch Hospital was volunteered as a reception centre for wounded servicemen brought back from France. Once just an infirmary serving the needs of the poor in the workhouse its role would be transformed by wartime demands. Marshalls, a minor mansion, was also commissioned to house recuperating invalids from the forces as the trickle of those wounded in the war became a flood. R.E. Giles remembered that during 'one of my mother's rare rest periods (she was like her colleagues, working at the infirmary military hospital almost continuously) she walked out with my sister and me. The wartime searchlight in Osborne Road, possibly the first in the district, installed on a piece of waste ground was the object of our visit. It was being tried out – what an innovation in a peaceful country town.' The outing was concluded by a surprise, as Giles notes. 'When we arrived back home, it was to find my father waiting outside an empty home, on leave from France. It was common during those troubled days after a long and appalling period in action for the survivors relieved by another unit, and in a condition to walk, to be sent home for a few days' leave. There were of course more doctors available to "vet" their state of health and approve their being sent back to the line.'

A group of wounded soldiers with friends. The war was notable for the loss of limbs in action. Soldiers would be sent to the new Roehampton Hospital to be fitted with early artificial replacements.

Dora Collier, who served as a nurse tending wounded soldiers in Romford, asked many of the troops to write or draw on a page of their autograph books. 'The Boy Scout captures a German spy' is one of the more humorous pages. Others contain poems, trying to put a cheerful gloss on their experiences in France, but often a sad note comes through. Many pages are signed at the bottom with such comments as 'Wounded at Loos – Saturday 25 September 1916' (Private S. McDonald), 'Wounded at Ypres – 30 July 1915' (9820 Lance Corporal Hankin, W., 2nd Oxford & Bucks Light Infantry). One comment below a jolly poem essays a venture into French: 'Blessé à Hoog près Ypres – 31 July 1915' (Corporal Fred A. Bean, Durham Light Infantry).

Trinity Wesleyan Church, 1915. The noticeboard on the right probably contains a Roll of Honour of those killed in the conflict in Europe.

4

Romford Comes of Age

T he war years had changed people's outlook in many ways. The need to send every fit, and many unfit, men to war in France and Belgium and, it is sometimes forgotten, to the Middle East, had created huge gaps in the labour market and the local economy. Although some older men, too old for National Service, came out of retirement the gaps could not be filled without the widespread recruitment of women. At one fell swoop many old barriers and prejudices against the employment of women in certain jobs were broken down. The male population of the Romford area, as in the rest of Britain, had plummeted through the tremendous casualties associated with winning the war. International trade was also in a bad way, especially in Europe where many towns had been almost completely destroyed. Before the war many German firms and individuals had played a part in industry and business in Britain and this sector had been removed through the internment or repatriation of these people and the seizure of some of their assets.

Thus Romford like everywhere else had to start afresh. The 1920s eventually saw the growth of new enthusiasm and opportunity for business and professional development, but it would take a few years for this to materialise. Many families had lost their original breadwinner; fathers and brothers and uncles had all perished in the conflict. Some damage had been sustained in Britain by air attacks but Romford had avoided nearly all of these. At the end of the war in 1919 the flu pandemic killed many local people already worn out by wartime deprivation and anxiety.

However even while the war was still going on, at home some individuals not called to war were planning the future. In the *Romford Recorder* of 6 March 1915 an article under the heading 'Some civic ideals; food for serious thought' recorded ideas thrown up by a meeting at the Mawney Road School, the object of which was to support the candidature of Mr T. England for a seat on the urban council as a member for the Collier Row ward. Ideas discussed involved improvements to danger spots in the road system; the need for a town hall, a library and other public buildings; improvements to the sewage farm; new parks laid out attractively and the creation of a technical institute. England himself referred to the housing question and pointed out the scheme adopted by Ilford Urban District Council: 'they granted loans up to £400 at 4% to householders who wished to buy their own freehold, and the legal charges and survey charges were very slight. If a man wanted to buy a £250 house, and could put down £50, the balance of £200 was loaned at 4%, and the payment of £2 and sixpence per month for 10 years would make the house the property of the householder. Already the Ilford Council had arranged 500 mortgages under this scheme.' This was certainly of interest to better-paid Romfordians, many of whom were still renting their houses, and might be seen as a first step in encouraging more widespread home ownership backed by a progressive council.

Left: These immaculately turned-out girls were pupils at the Romford County High School, and by the 1930s were able to take advantage of a new breed of young women teachers being trained in institutes of teacher education. The young teacher seen here probably came from outside the town, impressed by its growing attractions as a shopping and entertainment venue. Surprisingly, the County High School for Girls had begun in 1960, based on a previous private academy, the Claughton House School in Eastern Road. It was another 15 years before a boys' grammar school was set up in the old Hare Hall. This was the Royal Liberty School; before its advent boys from Romford had usually been sent by ambitious parents to Brentwood Grammar School.

Below: Romford Market in the 1920s appeared to carry on in many ways along the old pattern, but appearances were deceptive. In this view there are many farmers and dealers of livestock as before, but Romford was beginning to appeal to a wider cross-section of the public. There were still horse slaughterers and under the arch on the far side was a blacksmith, but in small offices in the market and around the town, a new breed of professionals was appearing: accountants, solicitors and estate agents were increasing in numbers. Though horse collars, leather goods and basketware still proclaimed the importance of agriculture in the general market, more everyday items for the home were being sold. At the far end the Laurie Hall has housed a cinema since 1913. Castles printing works and the Globe Dining Rooms are prominent on the north side of the market. The Romford Shopping Hall will not be built until the next decade – Romford still has some catching up to do on the retail front.

Romford post office had been rebuilt in a fairly modern style at the beginning of George V's reign, in a good position on what was to become the principal shopping street. The outside of the building at the upper level is still recognisable, with its George V monogram high up. In this early picture it stands out, awaiting the development of two houses beyond, which will create an unbroken run of shops, together with those built on the site of the White Hart field or Hoppit after 1902. This previous terrace had persuaded several national companies such as Sainsburys, Lush & Cook's the cleaners and Barclays Bank to occupy a prominent position in the street. The telephone exchange was established in this building when the business of the private National Telephone Company was transferred to the GPO in 1912. When in 1915 a new exchange was needed it was the most modern of its type in the Greater London area.

A high point in Bedfords Park: Romfordians enjoy a picnic. Far-sighted councillors and locals campaigned for this country park to be purchased in the 1930s before house building could occur. The borough, when it came into being in 1937, inherited a fine legacy of open spaces large and small, from Laurie Square Gardens opened in 1920 (the first to be added after Raphael Park) through to a last-minute donation of Rise Park, in 1937.

This telephone exchange behind South Street dated from 1931. When it opened there were 1,128 lines. In 1936 there were 50 public telephone kiosks in the area. The building suffered damage in the Second World War, on the night of 13/14 October 1940, yet the service was only interrupted for 39 minutes. More seriously, on 8 December that year it received a direct hit during an air raid and part of the building was demolished, resulting in the death of one telephonist. This exchange was enlarged in 1960 and a completely new building further down South Street took over a couple of decades later. However this building remained in Exchange Street until the brewery behind it closed and the Brewery Shopping Centre was created.

This unusual viewpoint shows the balcony and interior walls of a house in Heath Drive, still displaying the full architectural credentials of the International style, built during the 1934 Modern Homes Exhibition – a second part of the Gidea Park Estates development after an interval of twenty years.

The Plaza cinema entrance stands out clearly where today is an entrance to the Liberty Shopping Centre. This cinema, designed by the architects Harrington & Evans, opened on 20 January 1930 with the films *They Had to See Paris* and *The Girl from Havana*. The town was getting a 'modern' aspect and the whole of South Street above the station and even below became very prosperous and known as the Golden Mile. The shops beyond the cinema can still be identified as those built after this side of South Street was widened in the 1930s.

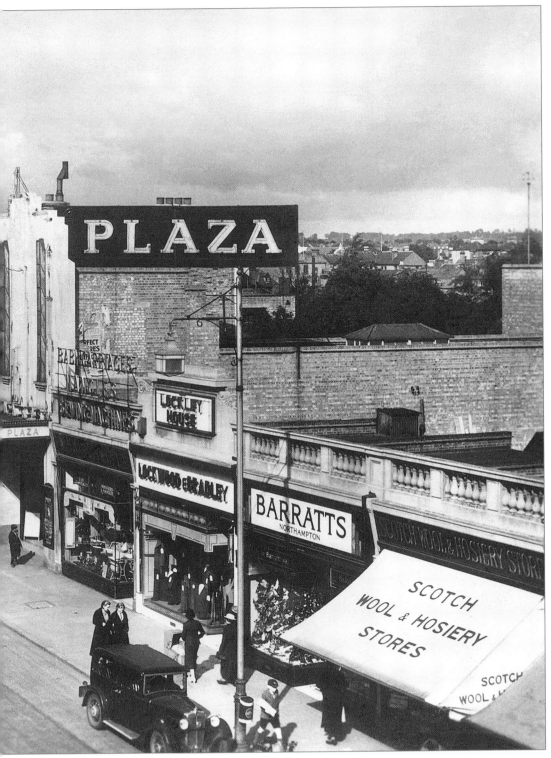

A.F. Thompson remembered that opposite the Barclays Bank parade of shops above the Plaza, 'Bartons occupied a frontage of about 40 feet. The Barton brothers operated a thriving clothiers and haberdashers shop. But with supertax at nineteen shillings and sixpence in the pound, immediately after the war, Barton said he resented earning only sixpence for every pound, and he sold up when the Golden Mile commanded over £1,000 per foot frontage – a pitiful sum by today's reckoning.'

On 16 September 1937 a police sergeant keeps a watchful eye as Charles Allen, Mayor of Romford, stands with Sir George Broadbridge, the Lord Mayor of the City of London, who prepares to make a speech from the dais erected outside St Edward's Church. Romford had become a borough, the culmination of many years' development, and is receiving its royal charter from the Lord Mayor. Romford is coming closer to becoming a part of the great metropolis. But Broadbridge did not want to offend and said that 'it was pleasing to note that Romford would retain much of its original character as a self-contained township'.

Romford's first Lady Mayor, Lilian Irons, inspecting members of local service organisations, accompanied by the Lord Lieutenant of Essex, Colonel Whitmore, at the War Memorial Old Folks' Club, Eastern Road, 1953–4.

5

Leisure

In the early twentieth century leisure time was very restricted owing to long working hours and absence of the white goods that now master many domestic chores, like washing, cleaning and cooking. Expectations were simpler then, and children enjoyed very basic toys, such as wooden and metal farmhouse models, comics and books, and living in the world of their imagination. Adults created entertainment sitting round the piano at home, singing popular songs. People thought nothing of walking out with the children, even toddlers in prams, through miles of country roads, armed only with a picnic. Adults also enjoyed the music hall or variety theatre, with its collection of performers. Romford never had a proper music hall, but there was, in Edwardian times, a wooden and canvas construction on the field at the bottom of Victoria Road where such performances took place. After it burned down people travelled by train to the Ilford Hippodrome. The cinema came early to Romford, with the adapted Laurie cinema, which survived until after the Second World War. A second cinema in South Street became the Victory after the First World War. Providing entertainment at a rather basic level for many years, they were supplanted in the 1930s by the super cinemas mentioned below. Today entertainment is seen in larger terms and vast amounts of money are spent on this leisure pursuit inside and outside the home.

In the mid-twentieth century the number of licensed houses declined, but a new breed of drinking places, where male and female can freely mix, have increased the drinking population in the town. In fact Romford is seen as a mecca for visitors, intent on enjoying the great variety of clubs, pubs and night-time venues.

It is interesting to get the viewpoint of youngsters still at school on Romford's leisure scene: 'All these people need nightlife, so there are plenty of pubs, clubs and restaurants' (*Stephanie Aldis*); 'I think Romford's entertainment is quite good, but it's very expensive, (*David Wilson*). Other types of leisure activity are of great interest to young people: 'The Dolphin swimming pool closed ages ago and now they are to build an Asda, which is really bad because there are too many shops' (*Stephanie Jarman*); 'My earliest memory of Romford is of going to the cinema for the first time with my dad at the old Odeon cinema. [Today] the entertainment is very satisfying, with the bowling alley, the cinema and the Brewery, I manage to keep myself entertained. The parks are exquisite, they offer great entertainment without the cost, and there are plenty of them' (*Kieran Richardson*); 'My earliest memory of Romford is that when I was two years old I used to go to the Dolphin swimming baths with my parents, and attended a club there called Mini-Movers' (*Luke Tisser*); 'I do think that the Romford area has been spoilt because the Dolphin swimming centre is being demolished after not being a building for very long' (*James Long*); 'My earliest memory of Romford is when I went ice skating when I was ten' (*Sam Brown*); 'I think the entertainment is good and there's lots of it . . . it makes Romford more interesting' (*Tina Tayeby*).

At the sides of the Time & Envy nightclub foyer today, the amazing double staircase of the original Havana cinema, opened on 29 January 1936, still exists. This was the second of Romford's three modern film theatres, all built in the golden age of cinema-going, the 1930s. The final cinema was the Ritz at 178 South Street. The Havana, which later gave its name to a car park, was renamed the Odeon, and is the only one of the three buildings still standing.

Opposite, above: In 1905 Mawney Road Baths had only been open for a few years. It was one of Romford's earliest leisure amenities, and heavily used by schoolchildren, who walked to it in crocodiles from all over town. Adults came from a great distance in some cases, and several swimming and water polo clubs were started here. In the early years the boarded-over baths provided an alternative public hall for the town to complement the Corn Exchange in the High Street, where public meetings and 'smoking concerts' were held.

Opposite, below: Feeding sparrows in Raphael Park in the 1950s, with an excellent view of the historic bridge that carries Main Road over the lake. Romford had joined the ranks of the municipally advantaged when it acquired Raphael Park, mostly through the generosity of Herbert Raphael at the beginning of the twentieth century. When some other plots had been added and new planting undertaken, it became, and remains today, a unique asset to the town.

Right: An advert of 4 December 1936, giving details of events at the Nimbus. Ballroom and other types of dancing were a great pastime in Romford in the 1930s. Each ballroom had its own type of clientèle. The Wykeham Hall was a superior venue, the ballroom high above the Quadrant Arcade (later the Shannon) attracted nurses and friends from Oldchurch Hospital, and there were many others. The Nimbus building, on several storeys, stood at the top end of the market, near the entrance to today's pedestrian underpass. It was certainly quirky, as the wording here shows. A crooning competition (Frank Sinatra and others had made this singing style popular), a hair perming machine demonstration, a café, tea dances and Lady Standing's beauty preparations were all available in this one establishment. This is the kind of surprising conjunction that visitors and locals enjoyed about the town.

NIMBUS

BALLROOM

96, Market Place

ROMFORD

Telephone:
ROMFORD 707

TO - MORROW (SAT.)

CROONING COMPETITION

DANCING 8—12 :: 2/-

BALLROOM
CLASSES
MONDAYS &
TUESDAYS
7 10.30

ADVANCED
BEGINNERS
JUNIORS
and
CHILDREN

Principal : Mrs. F. DRAKE-LAW, M.I.S.T.D.
(Ballroom Branch, Honours)

TEA DANCES EVERY THURSDAY

3.30—5.30   1/6 including Tea

NIMBUS CAFE

MORNING COFFEE
LUNCHEONS, TEAS, Etc.

THURSDAY, DEC. 10

From 7 to 10 p.m.

FREE

DEMONSTRATION

OF THE
WELLER RAPID PERMANENT
WAVING MACHINE
AND

LADY STANDING'S

BEAUTY PREPARATIONS

In the 1930s radio had become the big entertainment in the home. The wireless sets of the time were monster boxes with complicated innards, tending to make a delightful whistling sound as the dial was tuned to a particular station. Taking the back off revealed large valves which lit up like bulbs, and 101 other components.

COSSOR SERIES "58" All-wave SUPERHETS
Incorporating CONTROLLED BAND-WIDTH TUNING • NEW WIDE - RESPONSE MOVING - COIL SPEAKER • SPECIALLY MATCHED HIGH - SLOPE OUTPUT • DIODE DETECTION WITH FULL DELAYED AUTOMATIC VOLUME CONTROL

In 1953, coronation year, this theatre group with the full cast of *The Sport of Kings* appears on stage in costume.

Romford Drama and Operatic Society, 1950s. Archie Baker, a keen member of such groups, sits in the centre of the front row (he is the one with Prince Charles-like ears). Romford has had a very strong tradition of amateur dramatic productions and theatre groups, but has never had its own proper theatre. Until the 1970s there were several schools of dancing, speech and drama for young people. Raphael Park since the Second World War has had a dedicated area where the Summer Theatre performs a Shakespeare play annually.

Above: These smiling faces belong to the members of the YMCA, pictured by the tennis courts in the old YM premises west of North Street in the grounds of an old house, summer 1939. This site was later occupied by the postal sorting office, now a large retail outlet. A very famous sportsman of his time is on the far right of the back row. Johnny Leach was one of England's top table tennis players, and became world champion at the sport. Even on relaxed social occasions people still wore very formal clothes, only one or two bucking the trend.

Left: A group of brewery workers lines up for the photographer outside the social club by the Woolpack, off Romford High Street. They are waiting for the coach to take them on a one-day beano – a trip to the coast with crates of beer in the boot, and a stop at a number of public houses along the way: what you might call today a male bonding exercise.

Right: Eating, dancing and cavorting! Romford's new type of bar/entertainment centre/nightclub for the twenty-first century. This was, not so long ago, Romford's post office and the royal cipher of George V can still be seen high up on the front elevation.

Getting a bet on before the race starts: an atmospheric scene at Romford's Greyhound Racing Track and Stadium, London Road, 1930s. This venture, started by Archer Leggett and Michael Pohl, began in 1929 on the other side of London Road. Archer Leggett had a real showman's flair which he used to good effect in business as well as charity events. He was President of Romford Rotary Club 1948–9, second i/c 4th Battalion Home Guard (Essex Regiment) and later Deputy Lord Lieutenant of Essex.

6

Transport

In 1905 Romford was still dominated by horse transport. This included the taxis at the station, which were usually run by the proprietor of the Star Hotel. At this time, and for some time to come, fields started halfway up North Street and there was no Eastern Avenue, so the street continued northward as a country lane, with few houses along its length. Victorian houses had been built north of where the Parkside Hotel now stands, and along Hainault Road where it forks to the left. Miss P.A. Corbell has memories of her mother coming to the ivy-covered house that until recently stood at the junction with Eastern Avenue, at the start of the 1920s.

'Coming to live in the country was how they thought of it. All round the town were fields of corn or meadows with cows and horses. We lived about a mile from the market town, in a house with fields and animals opposite, and the lane to Havering outside, three miles away across the fields and lanes. There were horse buses from Romford station at first, only later the petrol buses. But soon the main road to London came (in 1925) and took part of our garden, so now instead of animals and fields we had a dual carriageway to Southend. This soon brought trippers to and from Southend every weekend in their cars. In summer other people used to make it an evening treat to sit and watch them coming home, from the side of the road. In those days the baker, milkman, grocer, butcher and laundryman all called at the house, delivering every week, so one didn't go shopping as regularly as today. Only on market days would we go and buy from the many stalls and see the animals in the pens – calves, pigs, sheep, cows and bulls. What a scare when one of them escaped, chased by the drovers and farmers the length of the market!'

John Hewitt remembered the gradual change from horse to motor vehicles, although some horses remained on the streets until after the Second World War. 'At the General Election in 1906 I had my first ride in a motor car. It was a Darracq. We drove from the Congregational Chapel in South Street (Abbey National stands there now) up as far as where the new Territorial Army depot was to be (and where I joined the local army battery on 3 October 1914), near Oldchurch Road. Then we turned back again, and as we passed the corner of Victoria Road, I shouted above the din to ask the chauffeur what speed we were doing. With a touch of pride he shouted back: "We must be doing at least 25." This same rather good-looking chauffeur drove the first Romford taxi, a green Unic, a French make. It was powered with a vertical twin engine, and going up Victoria Road the driver always had to change down just before reaching Princes Road – and what a clashing of gears! Then the local doctors bought cars: Eric Wright had a single-cylinder 8-horsepower Rover, with the gear lever on the steering column; his cousin Sam Wright had a green Humber; Dr Ryan had an American Hudson, I believe; and Dr Upward had a De Dion Bouton, also a single-cylinder car. Soon South Street often had a car standing somewhere by the kerb. One day there was a cream 60-hp Napier. It had just beaten the world record for the flying half mile at 60 mph.'

Arthur Gilbert was a young lad when his father left his car outside Symons the solicitors in South Street, and he with it. Without ado Arthur carefully turned it round in the road. On his father's return much amazement was caused as to how this could have happened. Even at that young age, Arthur was learning all about motors. He later set up a car sales business with his brother.

This is what young people think of transport facilities in Romford today:

'The local transport system is OK since the buses kind of run on time, but sometimes you get out of service buses . . . the trains are quite reliable since they do go where they say they are going, and most of them run on time – it's just that they are not the cleanest way to get around' (*Samantha Curran*); 'Getting buses at the weekend takes ages sometimes, because if you miss your bus, you may have to wait another half hour or more for another one. Inside the buses it is a bit sticky. There is graffiti and stuff on the walls – although taking the bus is quicker than walking'

(*Kathryn Grant*); '[Romford] has direct links to London that are very convenient for people working or living out of London' (*Amy Porter*); 'The transport system is a big time-saver as long as you don't mind the sound of noisy teens and the smell of cigarettes' (*John Kelly*); 'Romford station now has a café on the platform, and there are more bus stops to provide easy transportation in and out of town. The A12 passes through town, enabling easy access to the M25' (*Daniel Ong*).

Many pupils at school today have little experience of public transport as they are taken by car by their parents or others.

This advert shows what taxicabs looked like in a very early form, before and at the start of the First World War. The first taxicab licence issued by Romford Urban District Council for a motorised vehicle is Plate No. 1 issued on 4 January 1911 to A. Martin, who paid the grand sum of one shilling. This licence lasted for one year, and the documents stated 'the Driver's Badge is the property of the Council, and must be delivered to the Council's Inspector when the Driver ceases to act as such, or is leaving the neighbourhood'.

Private and commercial vehicles in the Market Place, early 1930s. Note the delivery bike casually laid down on the kerb – no need to chain it up. The Neville's bread van in the right distance appears to be parked outside Humphrey's café – a very well-known local institution, where the customers sat in booths, as in many eating houses of the time. One of Romford's coach-like buses can be seen in the middle distance. Is this a City or Hillman's vehicle? A mother and her child appear to be prospective passengers, and it can be seen that people had to wait a long way back on the pavement, in imminent peril of being knocked down.

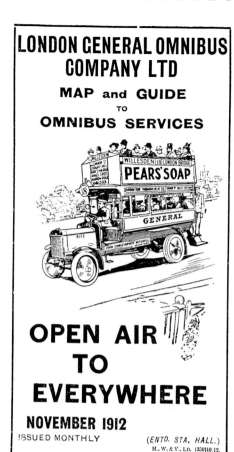

LONDON GENERAL OMNIBUS
COMPANY LTD

MAP and GUIDE
TO
OMNIBUS SERVICES

OPEN AIR
TO
EVERYWHERE

NOVEMBER 1912
ISSUED MONTHLY

(ENTD. STA. HALL.)
H., W., & V., LD. (350)10.12.

The style of the early 'boneshaker' buses operated by the largest operator, London General Omnibus Company, is illustrated on this map and guide of 1912.

A bus belonging to Romford & District Motor Services. L.A. Thomson in the eighth issue of the *Romford Record* mentions that 'during the twenties several services were started in the Romford area, but as they did not penetrate the metropolitan district they carried no service numbers. . . . The Romford & District ran three services from Mawneys (Eastern Avenue) via Mawneys Road and South Street, Victoria Road, Albert Road and Brentwood Road to Noak Hill, also to Harold Wood and to Emerson Park, using red 20-seater vehicles. The proprietors were Messrs Roberts and Hammer.'

The 370 Romford to Grays route is still running today, operated by Arriva Southend. This image shows a double-decker on the route in London Transport-operated days. When the London Transport Passenger Board took over in a rationalisation of services on 1 July 1933, the route was called the G40 and originally dated from the late 1920s, when it was started by the National Omnibus Company.

On a quiet non-market day in 1961, this view includes a bus shelter on the far left, looking a bit like a cattle shed. This again shows how the pedestrian had to get to the bus stop on busy days while risking life and limb, since cars were now allowed to park on the market plain by St Edward's Church.

In 1949 a real country bus, the 238, served the Pentowan Café, Noak Hill, a destination still shown on service vehicles (long after the café had closed) in the 1970s.

Heady days for passenger transport in Romford's Golden Mile. Possibly eleven buses can be seen attempting to negotiate a passage through the logjam caused by sheer weight of numbers of passengers boarding at the bus stops along the street. Nearer to the camera are Eastern National's 2A service to Southend, and London Transport's 66A and 247. A wooden direction post still stands on the left, and the Westminster Bank across the road is still in its one-storey premises, which were vacated in 1964 to permit the building of the modern banking hall.

South Street in the 1950s, looking towards the post office on the left and what is by this time the Gaumont (previously the Plaza). On this occasion shopping crowds line the pavements, but the pace of life seems quite gentle. Only one bus is visible at the moment the photographer captures the scene. During these years Romfordians could alight from a vehicle in the middle of South Street, pop into Sainsbury's, post a letter at the post office, cross to Marks & Spencers, and be back on the bus going home in 20 minutes!

In 2002 the scene is transformed. With the pedestrianisation of the same street, shoppers again stroll casually. The stress comes when they return to their cars, with ever busier roads, parking, confusing road signs and the whole paraphernalia of travelling anywhere today. In spite of the increase in road space, the population of Romford is larger and many more are travelling to work in the town with the great increase in shops and services.

Only two lines served Romford station before 1930, when two new fast lines were added. This nostalgic photograph shows the station as it was with passengers waiting for a steam train to puff its way into the platform. An iron bridge connected the up and down lines, and the rather unusual pattern of underground slopes, passages and stairways had not yet been created.

Left: Here is the old-fashioned brick arch that carried the two lines over South Street, seen *c.* 1905, many years before the transformation of the arch into steel bridges, described as a triumph of British engineering when it was carried out overnight in 1930. At this time the Upminster branch was operated by a different railway company from the main line, and its separate station is seen on the left. There was, however, a separate passenger bridge for transfer between the lines: this is seen extending above the arch.

Inset: On 13 August 1949 loco 58038 awaits departure from Romford Platform 1 bound for Emerson Park and Upminster. In the 1960s the Beeching Report on the future of railways would threaten to close down this useful service at the very time that road journeys were getting longer. Four minutes to Emerson Park, and another four to Upminster, make this a fast connection between important centres. The old-fashioned gas lamps, telegraph poles and wooden platform contrast oddly with the modern frontage of what was then Times Furnishing, seen under the wires of the DC electrified main line. Peter Crollie, who lived in a house backing on to the line in the 1950s, remembered that his mother and other housewives objected to the smuts from the steam engine soiling the washing hanging out to dry.

The 'Flying Scotsman' in Romford. One of a series of exhibitions held in the 1930s by the London & North Eastern Railway occurred at Romford on 6/7 June 1936. From 9 a.m. to 9 p.m. Romfordians flocked to view locomotives, Pullman cars, sleeping cars, camping coaches, in total 64 different attractions. And where was space found for all this equipment? At the time, and until the latter decades of the twentieth century, extensive coal yards and sidings existed on the site of the present Hollywood nightclub and reached as far as the bus station; this was the location for this spectacular show. Excited crowds, including many children, spent the whole day sampling the delights, which included a 'guessing the weight of a piece of coal' competition – the winner to receive a quarter of a ton of coal. Most houses were then heated by coal fires.

After the rebuilding of the station in 1930 the booking office on the right-hand side of the ground floor as travellers entered from South Street, which looked like a railway carriage itself, remained in use until 1976. The photograph shows the new automated office constructed on the left-hand side. With the advance in computerisation of ticketing and the need for income in station retail units, the next change came in less than two decades when a further modernisation moved the ticket office on to a mezzanine floor. It is now hard to remember that the original ticket offices of the first half of the twentieth century still continued the nineteenth-century practice of using 1,000 ticket stocks, each pre-printed with a different destination, class of travel and type of concession (e.g. workman's; early morning; cheap day and so on) involving the clerks in a selection process from the serried racks around the office as they dealt with each customer.

The first day of a new air route to Paris: the inaugural flight from Romford Aerodrome. Edward Hillman (lower left) had by the 1930s built up a service of buses running from Bow, through Romford and along the A12, some even reaching into East Anglia. Late in 1931 he met up with former Air Force pilot Harold 'Timber' Wood, and his transport ambitions now focused on civil aviation. Signing up Wood as his chief pilot, he changed the name of his firm to Hillman's Saloon Coaches and Airways Ltd, on 12 November 1931. He now proposed to carry by air the kind of passengers who used his coaches (i.e. the man in the street, who would not at this time ever have thought of travelling by air). He believed they would be attracted by cheap fares and convenient services. The obvious choice for an airfield was Maylands at Harold Wood (the same name as his pilot!), just north-east of Romford, which had been established in 1928 for pleasure flights.

Later Hillman moved to Abridge, also known as Essex Airport, Stapleford, and ran further services to Ostend, Brussels, Glasgow, Belfast, Liverpool, Manchester and Thanet. Quite an expansion from his original flights which went to Clacton.

A cheerful bunch of staff members from Messrs Edwards and Co., Provisions, Plaistow, anticipate a thrilling day out by air to Clacton, setting a new benchmark for staff outings, in August 1932. The 45-mile trip to the seaside was achieved in 25 minutes via Hillman's Airlines.

Just before the Second World War in 1938 these women pilots were preparing for the first All-Women Pilots' Display at Romford Aerodrome. A magazine article of the time reported that 'the proportion of women pilots in Britain is actually rather low – in November 1937 there were only 196 out of a total of 4,724 who held "A" licences – but the number is increasing rapidly. . . . At the Romford Flying Club there is an enthusiastic band of girls taking instruction in the art of flight, and very attractive they look too in their white overalls.' These overalls were supplied by a firm called Wayfarer Tailored Clothes.

7

Shopping's Golden Days

In earlier centuries most of the buying and selling of goods would have taken place on the Market Square. Bargains would be struck on the market plain and in the public houses which surrounded it. As there were few shops, some traders would hire rooms in the inns and houses along the sides. The earliest directories of the late eighteenth century show the beginning of today's retail heaven, fuelled by the horse coaches that stopped in the town on their way between London and East Anglia. Romford's shopping area continued to grow through the nineteenth and early twentieth centuries, after which it became the dominant feature of the town. Until the second half of the nineteenth century shops were confined to the Market Place and the High Street, and even by 1905 South Street's lower half still contained many large houses with long gardens in front. Edwardian Romford saw the beginning of a boom in new shops, and it was at this time that visitors began to have a dual reason for coming to Romford – not only to see the animals and traders on the plain, but also to seek out the varied merchandise available in the other streets. Some of the important local traders of 1905 have long since vanished, mostly killed off by the competition of national multiple traders in the twentieth century. A favourite phrase today is to say that the main streets of every sizeable town all contain the same trading names.

But in 1905 there were many local retail businesses, trying to harness the new skills of advertising and promotion in the local newspaper, local directories, of which few have survived, and even on public transport. Some of them were:

Aylett Bros, Family Butchers at 88/90 Market Place.
Daldy & Co., Coal and Timber Merchants at Romford Station Yard, etc.
Geo. Cooper, Pork Butcher in the High Street.
A.E. Davis, General and Fancy Draper at 2 Park Lane.
Poston Bros, Butchers at 52/54 High Street.
A.R. Tuff, Watchmaker & Jeweller at 13 South Street.
Dook & Dook, Food Specialist & Tea Men in Brentwood Road.
B. Wallis, Grocery and Provisions at 48 Market Place.
Edward Barten, General Draper at 43/45 South Street.
Evans & Wheatley, Ironmongers & Electric Bellworks at 22 Market Place.
J. Bower, Practical Saddler & Harness Maker in South Street.

There was also of course Stone's department store in the Market Place, which retained its name until the 1970s, although taken over by Debenhams. Today even some of the descriptions, such as drapers and grocers, are becoming redundant. It is interesting to remember that the huge Sainsbury business started as a small grocer in London.

Young people, girls and boys, have definite views on Romford's shopping facilities:

'There is a big variety of shops, but it gets very busy in Romford at the weekend' (*Sarah Russell*); 'Shopping in Romford is quite good but it can get a little crowded. There is a variety of shops and places to go' (*Courtney Harrison*); 'Shopping is very big in Romford. If it was an Olympic event, Romford would win the Gold. There are so many shops, bars, restaurants, cafés, department stores, rentals, leisure, super-markets – absolutely everything' (*Alex Phillips*); 'The shopping I think could be better – you don't always get what you want and there are too many fast food restaurants' (*Alfie Harper*); '[There are] plenty of shops but Romford can get very crowded' (*Alice Warren*); '[It is] every girl's dream, because it is within walking distance of everything; the shops, the market, the gym, all the hairdressers, the nail salons, the ice rink, the cinema, the bowling alleys and all the restaurants' (*Levi Thornton*); 'The shopping centre in Romford has improved massively in all kinds of ways like new shelter, more shops, etc.' (*Shanta Lall*).

The artist Dorothy Paton captured the east end of Romford's cattle market in this view of about 1930. This is where Romford's commercial power began, though at that time this area contained only the offices of cattle auctioneers, public houses and the premises of J.E. Frostick, a chimney sweep. The latter was a vital service when every house was heated by coal fires. Failure to clean a chimney could result in a serious fire if the accumulated soot caught light.

Above: The flags of the 1937 coronation year decorate the contrasting south side of the market, which now contained a run of shop premises broken only by the frontages of the several inns and public houses that existed here. The sheep market created a free show that was one of Romford's market day amusements.

Right: Another early twentieth-century business, now long gone.

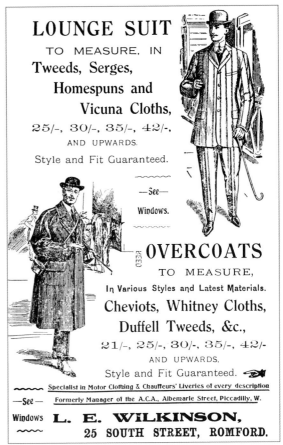

LOUNGE SUIT

TO MEASURE, IN

Tweeds, Serges, Homespuns and Vicuna Cloths,

25/-, 30/-, 35/-, 42/-,

AND UPWARDS.

Style and Fit Guaranteed.

— See —
Windows.

OVERCOATS

TO MEASURE,

In Various Styles and Latest Materials.

Cheviots, Whitney Cloths, Duffell Tweeds, &c.,

21/-, 25/-, 30/-, 35/-, 42/-

AND UPWARDS.

Style and Fit Guaranteed.

Specialist in Motor Clothing & Chauffeurs' Liveries of every description

— See —
Windows

Formerly Manager of the A.C.A., Albemarle Street, Piccadilly, W.

L. E. WILKINSON,
25 SOUTH STREET, ROMFORD.

In 1927 side streets still contained small shops like A.G. Godfrey at 119 Mildmay Road. The locals did not have to walk far to get their boots and shoes repaired.

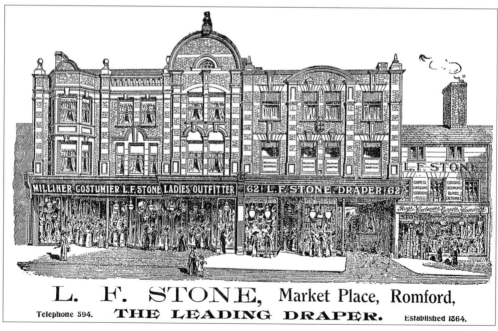

L.F. Stone's premises in the Market Place, early in the twentieth century when they were beginning to outgrow even their purpose-built premises and had taken over the former café on the right-hand side. They are still describing themselves as 'the leading draper' although they were already selling many items such as carpets, which did not fit into this category.

T.F. Collett's grocery shop, seen in about 1932, was detached from the premises on either side. His daughter Bessie told of how 'he had been manager of the original Sainsbury's in South Street, with a staff of eight people. After serving in the First World War he resumed his job in 1919. In 1922 he decided to set up in business for himself as a general grocer and acquired premises at 96 Market Place, which he stocked. Before he had really got started Sainsbury's produced a document which he had signed many years before, and forgotten about, to the effect that he would not open at any time a grocer's shop in the town in competition. To avoid problems he switched to greengrocery, which was not in Sainsbury's remit at that time. A friendly businessman Jimmy Craig guaranteed his setting up in business, and later another greengrocer, George Moore, who had a small shop in London Road often worked together with Collett in purchasing stock from Borough Market.'

A few shops in Balgores Lane backed on to those in Main Road facing the Unicorn public house. The Main Road parade had been built at about the time of the 1910/11 Exhibition of Houses. On the left is Green's Stores, part of a chain here in the 1920s. Note that Balgores Lane has not yet been properly kerbed.

This row of shops towards the station in South Street was built in about 1905. The balustrade along the top is very similar to that on another row still intact in South Street above Western Road, Romford, and another in Butts Green Road, Hornchurch. On the left-hand side nearest the camera there are still private houses with front gardens, later replaced by shops and now part of the bar/restaurant area.

Above: Romford Arcade in South Street brought a new shopping idea to the town. Along the front were shops like Craddock's which sold stationery, china and fancy goods, and in the words of their advert 'Distinctive notepapers; fountain pens of every make; account books and files; maps, guides and technical books; typewriter paper, carbon and ribbons; and rubber stamps'. Norman Stanley sold wireless apparatus (radio parts) and Jays was a druggist. Inside the arcade was Jays Arcade Library, a bookseller and the Romford Amusement Arcade. In the offices upstairs was the HQ of Romford Urban District Council, which occupied these premises for several years after the old courthouse building in the market had been abandoned before the new town hall, was opened in 1937.

Right: A view of the cattle market showing the old Pig in the Pound premises, and the original Shopping Hall which opened at the beginning of the 1930s and was Romford's second arcade. The proprietors described its advantages thus: 'pedestrian pressure on the street is reduced and the public can shop at leisure under cover and without the danger and noise of passing traffic. The shopkeeper has customers at his counter and is thus relieved of the demands on his time and space required by the conventional shop window.' At one time the name was changed to the Rumford Shopping Hall, in tune with the old name of the town.

Right: An amusing early twentieth-century advert for Taylor's off-licence. This business provided uplifting drinks for Romfordians during most of the century. Such businesses were overtaken by the large range of drinks available in many supermarkets in the closing decades of that century.

E. W. TAYLOR,
Wine, Spirit and Bottled Beers,
VICTORIA RD., ROMFORD.

WHAT IS IT MASTER LIKES SO MUCH?

WHAT WILL MASTER SAY!!

REID'S STOUT

REID'S STOUT

RIED'S STOUT	... ...	3/6 per doz.	2/- per crate (4 Flagons)
REID'S INVALID STOUT	3/- ,, ,,	1/6 ,, ,, ,, ,,
REID'S FAMILY STOUT	2/6 ,, ,, -	1/4 ,, ,, ,, ,,

Orders by Post delivered same day.   *A trial order respectfully solicited.*

Victoria Road junction with South Street has seen many changes since the 1950s, when Woodcraft's furniture store occupied the corner, and the Co-op Permanent Building Society (now Nationwide) the premises with the white upper storey. Keniston's motor cycles (still on the site) hold the record for longevity here. Jim Kirk remembers, 'this was a hot spot for furnishers, as well as Woodcrafts there was a second furniture store Killiwicks on the opposite corner to the right of the picture, and a third – Collyer's, in the premises across South Street, recently demolished, and taken over for housing. The strip of pavement on the far right where a lady shopper is walking, suddenly subsided at the end of the 1960s, opening up a large hole.'

At 2.30 p.m. on 23 September 1935 the new Quadrant Arcade was formally opened by Sir Philip Nash, chairman of Great Universal Stores. A large crowd of members of the public at both ends of the L-shaped passageway were temporarily held back but surged in, eager to view this new Romford wonder, which created a new thoroughfare between South Street and the Market Place.

Christmas started early even in 1936, when this 4 November newspaper advert reveals the simpler presents available in less affluent and credit card-less times.

A busy Quadrant Arcade seen from the Market Place entrance, 1980s.

This already nostalgic scene shows a 1980s view of the Liberty Shopping Centre, which created a whole new shopping area in the early 1970s on what had formerly been bowling green and 'backlands' inaccessible to the general public. One flagship firm which came briefly to serve Romford's hunger for shops was Gamages, but this was only a brief encounter. Many national names took up residence and have remained.

Opposite, above: These wandering minstrels celebrated Christmas in the early 1990s when Liberty 1 had been joined by Liberty 2, a shopping centre with a cinema and other facilities on several floors, built round a central atrium, and with escalators and feature lifts connecting the various levels. Part of Liberty 2 escalator system is seen at top right.

Opposite, below: Into the millennium and more shopping changes. What looks like a scene of war destruction is actually a grand reconstruction of the Liberty 1 centre, when building work continued month after month as shoppers picked their way through the hoardings and uneven floor levels.

The result in 2004 is a shinier shopping mall. The new roof affords visitors to the centre protection from the weather and drew favourable comment from the architectural broadcaster Maxwell Hutchinson on a recent visit. The large area of glass overhead and its intricate construction is reminiscent of the great plant houses at Kew Gardens. Romford also gained some new retail businesses.

8

Against the Odds . . .
& Hard Times

Romford's preparation for defence and shelter of the population began four years before the Second World War broke out. In fact, as Glyn Richards commented, 'as far back as 1935, when the Council, in common with all other local authorities, was asked to consider in very broad outline their plans for defence against air attack, with the saving clause that such measures in no way imply a risk of war in the near future and they are wholly precautionary. The initial Alert on 3 September 1939, which was actually a false alarm, as was that which sounded during the night of September 3–4, was followed by an alert about 7.30 a.m. on 6 September, during which an aeroplane passed over the town and a gun at the Whalebone Battery fired three or four rounds. There was much excitement and speculation during the day, and the general opinion was that the aeroplane was, in fact, a British one. Nevertheless Romford felt, somewhat proudly, that it had had its baptism of fire.'

What to do with the children? This for some time had been the question in the minds of most adults and of the government's collective mind. We have all heard of D-Day, but not so much about E-Day: this was evacuation day, 1 September 1939. Large groups of schoolchildren were sent almost willy-nilly from what were thought to be danger areas into the countryside, mostly by train, but sometimes by boat. Most mothers stayed behind, causing many scenes of heartbreak at the point of farewell. The children were accompanied by some teachers and there were some mothers who were evacuated. A total of 1,473,500 went to rural billets, according to official figures. This evacuation turned out to be premature as bombs did not drop for another eleven months. A second evacuation occurred with the onset of the Battle of Britain in the autumn of 1940 (starting in August). Blitzkrieg bombing had now spread a real fear of heavy casualties. During this time of savage air attack by the Germans there had already been considerable damge to property and many civilian deaths. So this evacuation of 1,250,000 women and children to rural parts must have saved many lives. The final evacuation was in 1944 when doodlebugs (pilotless planes) whose engines suddenly cut out, plunging them to the earth, appeared in mid-June. An exodus of over one million people (mothers, children, the elderly, invalids, pregnant women and hospital patients) fled mainly from London and the suburbs to escape this onslaught.

Colin Vale, who was aged between five and ten years during the war, remembers many incidents in wartime Romford. These included helping his father to dig the hole for the Anderson shelter; the appearance of sandbags everywhere to construct protective walls against blast; practising with gas masks (at only five years old he insisted on the 'grown-up' rather than the children's Mickey Mouse design); the excitement of the Dunkirk rescue, seen as a kind of victory, when many little boats brought back a large number of exhausted troops after defeat in France; watching aerial dogfights from the back garden; nightmares of the Nazis coming to shoot him, but hiding under the stairs; collecting shrapnel from the street (often while it was still warm); Air Raid Wardens shouting 'Put that light out' (all windows had to be effectively blacked out to prevent light escaping); taking classes in Mrs Tutt's front room after the school had been bombed, and teachers turned their homes into classrooms; the Home Guard (Dad's Army) exercising in Cottons Park, at first using mostly wooden rifles; seeing his windows blown in and rubble over his makeshift bed under the table while convalescing; watching his mother in the street during an air raid, using a long-handled rake and shovel for putting out incendiary bombs using sand; being aware of the mobile anti-aircraft gun moving through local streets. When it stopped and fired, it caused more damage and fear to the residents than the enemy; then the flying bombs (doodlebugs) arriving overhead, with the engine cutting out before crashing into the railway bank by Victoria Road.

And so in 1944 came the business of lining up in Bush Elms school playground where older brother Trevor was a pupil, over the border in Hornchurch. Then the order came and they were marched off for evacuation to an unknown destination. This turned out to be Llangollen in Wales, where the two brothers enjoyed a countryside childhood they would never have known but for the evacuation.

In 1944 many Romford schoolchildren were evacuated to Beccles in Suffolk. Brenda Matthews, who was a pupil at Heath Park Girls School remembers evacuation day: 'Motor coaches came to the school to take the children on the short journey to Romford railway station. We were accompanied by a teacher, Miss Mackie, and the headmaster, Mr Cocker. From the station the steam train journey to our destination in Suffolk seemed long and tiring. Pupils from Albert Road, Pettits Lane Boys and possibly Hylands Schools also took part in the evacuation. On arrival we went to a new area school. Prospective foster-parents gradually came and went, picking out children of their choice, a rather dispiriting process for those children who were left till last.' Eye-opening experiences included being rowed in a boat along the River Waveney, living in a hostel that had once been a chapel, and playing among the gravestones.

Finally the war was won, and there were VE (Victory in Europe) Day (officially 8 May) parties and bonfires everywhere. Later in the year the Japanese conflict also ended.

Barrage balloons hung in the sky over Romford and other towns along the route of the German bombers on their way to London. Writing a postcard to his nephew one correspondent said he had counted 56 balloons guarding the air space above.

The local newspaper which was not allowed to name the location in case it assisted the enemy captioned this picture 'What a bomb did in a residential road on Tuesday night. In the house on the right four people took shelter in a small room in the house, and had a miraculous escape from injury. In the foreground is a motor car overturned by the force of the explosion, and behind it is what remains of a house which met the full blast of the bomb.' The arbitrary way in which bombs and the blast effect affected people in a life and death situation gradually made wartime civilians fatalistic and the common phrase heard was 'If it's got your name on it there's nothing you can do'. The people in this house which was actually in Hill Grove were not sheltering in the approved manner, yet lived to tell the tale when the bomb fell overnight on 10/11 September 1940.

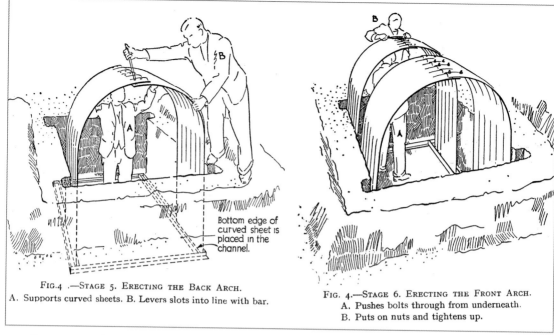

FIG. 4 .—STAGE 5. ERECTING THE BACK ARCH.
A. Supports curved sheets. B. Levers slots into line with bar.

Bottom edge of curved sheet is placed in the channel.

FIG. 4.—STAGE 6. ERECTING THE FRONT ARCH.
A. Pushes bolts through from underneath.
B. Puts on nuts and tightens up.

Instruction above – two stages for completing the construction of garden air raid shelters. Glyn Richards wrote, 'by August 1940, it was clear that the enemy would launch large-scale air attacks against London at any moment, and everyone was busy putting the final touches to the Anderson shelters and incorporating various ideas and comforts'. Lorna Poole remembers: 'When the Anderson steel shelters were issued in 1939 they were supposed to be installed in a hole 4 feet deep. No-one told the government the water-table round here was only 2 feet, so Dad dug the 2 feet and put a sump in one corner to pump out, piled the excavated soil on top and demolished the rockery to provide a little more cover.' The completed shelter is seen below.

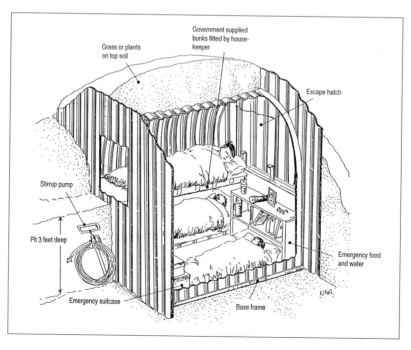

Grass or plants on top soil

Government supplied bunks fitted by house-keeper

Escape hatch

Stirrup pump

Pit 3 feet deep

Emergency food and water

Emergency suitcase

Base frame

FOOD FACTS

Five delicious dishes from one packet of dried eggs

Here are five different egg dishes which you can make from a single packet of dried eggs!

2½-minute Omelette

Omelettes are actually easier to make with dried eggs than they would be if you used shell eggs—and they take only 2½ minutes! Just the thing to serve for dinner or supper. They take the place of meat because eggs, you know, are also a protein food.

Scotch Eggs— new style

A really nourishing, tasty dish for supper, made with dried eggs, reconstituted and hard-boiled by steaming in greased egg-cups. Dried eggs are finest shell eggs with the shell and water taken away. White and yolk are blended together so you get the same even mixture every time.

Yorkshire Pudding

Another body-builder for the children, and a grand "filler" you can use to help out with potatoes. Light, golden brown, creamy in texture. It takes one egg, but the present allocation of dried eggs makes it possible for the average family to use a dozen eggs a week, which is more than most people used in peacetime!

New Treacle Tart

Ingredients: 6 oz. short pastry; 3 level tablespoons dried eggs, reconstituted; 3 level tablespoons syrup; a few drops lemon substitute. *Method:* Mix together eggs, syrup, and lemon substitute. Pour mixture into the pastry case and bake in a moderately hot oven for 20-30 minutes. Serve hot or cold. This can also be made into small tarts. It is a recipe the whole family will love.

Custard Sauce

Ingredients: 2 level tablespoons dried eggs, DRY; 2 level tablesps. flour, 1 level tablesp. sugar, 1 pint milk or milk and water, vanilla or almond flavouring. *Method:* Mix together egg, flour, sugar. Mix to smooth cream with a little of the milk. Boil rest of milk, pour on to mixture, return to pan and boil for 5 minutes. Add flavouring and stir well.

RECIPES for the omelette, Yorkshire Pudding, and Scotch Eggs are in recipe leaflets which you can have free of charge. Just write your name and address, in block capitals, on a postcard and send it to Leaflets Dept. P.W., Ministry of Food, London, W.1. Then you can show your family there's no egg shortage in *your* house!

Always measure dried eggs carefully — one level tablespoonful to two of water.

LISTEN TO THE KITCHEN FRONT ON TUESDAY, WEDNESDAY, THURSDAY AND FRIDAY at 8.15 a.m.

ISSUED BY THE MINISTRY OF FOOD, LONDON, W.1   FOOD FACTS No. 241

BEFORE, DURING AND AFTER THE RAID

A GOOD NIGHT'S REST IN THE PUBLIC SHELTER

—and the help that is ready if your home is hit

In public shelters some people spend the night far more comfortably than others. What is the secret of getting a good night's sleep? Here are some useful things to remember. These hints are taken from leaflets which are being issued to all shelterers.

BEDDING

Bedding should be aired daily, so that it keeps sweet and fresh. This daily airing will help to get rid of dampness. Put more blankets underneath you than on top of you. This is the best way to keep warm, and of course it is more comfortable.

GETTING TO SLEEP

Try not to lie on your back. You are less likely to snore if you lie on your side or front. You will rest better if you remove any heavy outer clothing before lying down. The shelter will get warmer as the night goes on, and you will need your warm outer garments when you go out into the early morning air.

CHILDREN

Before going to the shelter, dress children in night - wear rather than their other clothing. Then, when bed-time comes, you can simply take off the outer garments. They will not sleep well if they are too warm.

IN THE NIGHT

If you cannot sleep, or if you wake up, a warm drink will help.

Hot drinks keep fairly warm when wrapped in a blanket, though a hay-bottle is better. (See how to make a hay-bottle in the leaflet.) Keep something to eat beside you, in case you get peckish in the night.

Try not to make a noise late at night. You may keep others awake.

AFTER THE RAID
Have your plans made
Make plans now to go and stay with friends living near, but not too near, in case your house is destroyed. They should also arrange now to come to you if their house is knocked out. It's comforting to feel that everything is fixed up, just in case.

Help is ready
If your home is damaged, there is a great deal of help ready for you. Full arrangements have been made to give you food and shelter, clothes and money if necessary, and to find you somewhere to live. If you have not been able to make arrangements with friends, go straight to the emergency Rest Centre. The wardens and police know where it is. *Ask them.*

ISSUED BY THE MINISTRY OF HOME SECURITY

Information and advice on food and shelter was issued frequently in local newspapers and give-away leaflets, and played an important part in keeping people calm, because it appeared to show that the government was in control of the situation. The press did not complain about the nanny state in wartime! Two examples are shown here.

Public shelters were being provided by the government during the Phoney War period 1939–40 before the big air raids began. By the time the Battle of France in 1940 was over, according to Glyn Richards, there was 'accommodation for some 6,763 persons to be seated in these shelters. Subsequently, bunks were introduced to replace seats, and the accommodation accordingly reduced to provide sleeping space for 2,589 people.' A few examples remain today of the different types of shelter available at strategic points on the streets of Romford. The top picture shows the shelter built behind the wall of St Edward's Catholic presbytery, and the bottom picture shows the above ground entrance of the below ground shelter at Balgores Crescent/Balgores Lane.

A Romford War Savings Committee certificate presented to young Colin Vale during Warship Week in 1942 for a free expression pastel drawing of a warship, and signed by John Butterfield, Mayor of Romford. Many special savings weeks and collections were held, and it is quite surprising that in difficult wartime conditions people still put their hands in their pockets to contribute to these. Several campaigns were arranged as the war progressed to boost the flow of National Savings. 'Salute the Soldier', 'War Weapons Week' and 'Wings for Victory' were examples. Competition between towns was encouraged with large recording boards fixed on prominent buildings showing the savings total reached in each borough to spur on local savers. In Romford, for instance, a large wooden figure of a Tommy next to a representation of a thermometer was fixed to the Laurie Hall, the pointer moving upwards as a new total was achieved.

A parachute mine dropped from an enemy plane on Sunday 8 December 1940 severely damaged Romford telephone exchange, as can be seen in this photograph taken the morning after. The mine actually fell on top of the blacksmith's shop of S.H. Bush which was completely obliterated and the area all around littered with horseshoes and ironmongery. In the exchange 42-year-old Edward Fleming was found dead among the debris.

Left: The incident of 8 December also caused damage to the brewery buildings close behind the telephone exchange. Shops on South Street also felt the blast which incredibly lifted an anvil from the blacksmith's through the air over all the intervening buildings to land beyond the High Street in a brick shelter where seven people were sleeping. Incredibly, this only resulted in minor injuries, for it somehow came to rest in the empty bunk.

Below: This photograph shows the men and women of Nos 1 and 2 Light Rescue squads covering the Romford area. Mr J. Arnold remembered that women came to the fore again in this war, those pictured proving extremely tough and resilient drivers of rescue vans in the difficult conditions experienced during air raids. Typical problems occurred when the report centre in the basement of the town hall lost its means of communication on the night the telephone exchange was partly destroyed. The report centre was the central information and intelligence point and so on this occasion the heavy and light rescue squads could not be informed quickly of where help was needed and could not report back, except by using the slow system of messengers, who were themselves in danger of being killed or injured by bombs or shrapnel on their way. It could not have been a worse night for the report centre to be cut off – another parachute mine had fallen on the Air Raid Precautions depot in Oldchurch Road, destroying many of the rescue services vehicles and much equipment, required to deal with the other incidents before they could be deployed.

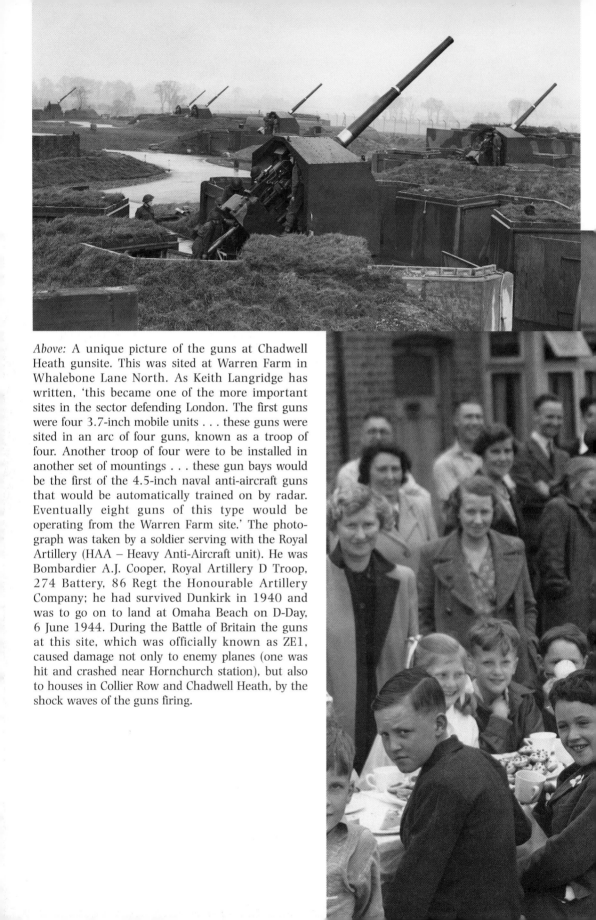

Above: A unique picture of the guns at Chadwell Heath gunsite. This was sited at Warren Farm in Whalebone Lane North. As Keith Langridge has written, 'this became one of the more important sites in the sector defending London. The first guns were four 3.7-inch mobile units . . . these guns were sited in an arc of four guns, known as a troop of four. Another troop of four were to be installed in another set of mountings . . . these gun bays would be the first of the 4.5-inch naval anti-aircraft guns that would be automatically trained on by radar. Eventually eight guns of this type would be operating from the Warren Farm site.' The photograph was taken by a soldier serving with the Royal Artillery (HAA – Heavy Anti-Aircraft unit). He was Bombardier A.J. Cooper, Royal Artillery D Troop, 274 Battery, 86 Regt the Honourable Artillery Company; he had survived Dunkirk in 1940 and was to go on to land at Omaha Beach on D-Day, 6 June 1944. During the Battle of Britain the guns at this site, which was officially known as ZE1, caused damage not only to enemy planes (one was hit and crashed near Hornchurch station), but also to houses in Collier Row and Chadwell Heath, by the shock waves of the guns firing.

Below: At last the war is over. Victory celebrations for the children at Birch Road off Mawney Road. The children sit at a long table by the kerb. Some of the plank seating is on trestles but the ubiquitous wartime sandbag has also been called into use in the absence of enough trestles. Joyful faces from the children and some of the younger mums but the strain of wartime life and bombing shows on the faces of a few of the older adults. Amid a record of the rejoicings, which included dancing in Raphael Park until midnight, illuminated by floodlights and fairy lamps, a local newspaper recorded 'there was no rejoicing in some hearts; the graveyards were bright with freshly laid flowers. On VE Day, the greatest day in the history of the present generation, many a silent tear was shed by mothers who had lost sons, and wives who had lost husbands in the war, and by relatives of people killed by enemy attacks on England.'

In the late 1940s and early 1950s shops like this in the Romford area put on a cheerful display. Not all the goods shown on the advertising cards were available, as much of this promotional material dated from pre-war times. This was a time of austerity which continued from the time that ration books were issued soon after the start of the war. By March 1940 bacon, sugar, butter and meat were being issued on a points system. In July 1940 rationing of tea started, and later, in 1941, jam, cheese, canned food and other groceries were additions to the list. Clothes began to be rationed from June 1941, and finally sweets from 1942. Although there were some relaxations, and certain goods were taken off rations, points or coupons, when the war ended, sweets were not finally taken off ration until early 1953, just in time for the coronation of Queen Elizabeth II. In wartime and after people often ate cough sweets as a substitute for chocolate bars and market stalls sold home-made candies like coconut ice. Now forgotten Fry's Punch, a concoction of chocolate, caramel and fudge, anticipated the end of rationing. New chocolate treats on the scene were Bounty, trialled in 1951 and released in 1955; Wagon Wheels in 1954; Picnic and Galaxy in 1958.

A scene in Romford's Market Place in the early 1960s. The people are bundled up in rather heavy clothes, a sight not so common today, when most people travel by car rather than public transport. More Romfordians still lived near the town centre, before supermarkets and car parks had eaten into the old housing areas. Notice the packet of Omo washing powder on the smart baby's pram. Mr Bloom, an American-style entrepreneur, was selling new washing machines on hire purchase to a large section of the population nationwide, using personable young salesmen knocking on front doors. There were one or two local shops selling prams and nursery furniture, such as Berman's Stores at 14 High Street, with brands like Silver Cross and Marmet. Outlets such as Mothercare and Children's World were yet to appear on the scene.

9

Changing Romford

Romford never stops changing, but up to the late 1960s the town still retained a number of interesting historical buildings, which were swept away as planners juggled the map of Romford, creating the first part of the ring road and the first Liberty Shopping Centre. Buildings out of scale with the traditional town such as Mercury House and North House started a trend towards concrete canyons, and developers still seem to want more.

Schoolchildren in Romford have comments to make. Surprisingly, younger teenagers already have a reminiscence span, and also hold opinions about changing Romford, the present and the future:

'The earliest memories I have of Romford are before the Liberty was covered over and when the Brewery was just that! When it rained we had to dash from shop to shop as there was no real shelter. None of the buses had low floors then, so Mum had to fold the pushchair to get on; what a hassle that was!' (*Jennifer Jones*); 'My earliest memories of Romford are the smell of the marketplace and the constant business of people going about their lives. As a small child this was interesting for me to watch. The smell however is my earliest memory; that putrid smell of rotting vegetables and the scent of fresh fish in the early morning' (*Jason Frost*); 'I believe that Romford is a better place than five or ten years ago, due to the renewal of the Brewery [area]. The new building work has changed Romford for the better' (*Luke Redpath*).

But some changes are unwelcome:

'[Romford has been spoilt by] People dropping litter and chewing gum on the floors. The traffic is also shocking in Romford – because of the Brewery more people are going to Romford' (*Dean Williams*); 'The area is modern [but] the prices have risen a lot' (*Chelsea Putnam*); 'Romford has been spoilt by vandals destroying things and doing graffiti' (*Andrew Jones*); 'I do think the area has been spoilt because there is litter on the floor everywhere. The roads are crammed and polluted' (*Jessica Day*).

Many young people have a love/hate relationship with the town:

'The reason I think [Romford] is bad is because of the gangs of hooligans that go round at night. The reason I think it is good is because of the entertainment, e.g. the bowling, cinema and shopping centres' (*Sandy Ortanca*); 'Many people are not happy with the design of Romford as it is very inconvenient, e.g. it has roundabout after roundabout. But despite all this I still love Romford as it is my home' (*Abbie Payne*); 'The people that make up Romford; some people are very troublesome and like to cause havoc – on the other hand people can be polite and kind, making Romford a better place to live in' (*Mathew Esan*); 'I think the pollution in the area is extremely bad . . . I know this sounds strange but without the odd smell and cough Romford wouldn't be the same' (*David Waters*).

These youngsters are thinking about Romford's nature and future:

'My earliest memories of Romford are the market and the now demolished brewery factory. I also remember the Dolphin swimming centre which is now being refurbished into an Asda shopping centre' (*James Jefferson*); 'I think that Romford is better now [than 5 or 10 years ago] because of its wide range of entertainment . . . [but] spoilt a little because of the Dolphin being closed down' (*Marshalls Park pupil*); 'My earliest memory of Romford is when I used to live in Oldchurch Road and I learned to ride in the park behind my house. Since then Romford has changed dramatically in shops, parks and schools. Romford has become more popular since the Brewery Centre has been built. I would miss it if I ever had to move away' (*Andrew Lewis*); 'I think Romford means a relaxing place where everything is . . . Brewery Centre, ice rink and hospitals' (*Jasdev Hathi*); 'They wanted people to come to the town. So they replaced the beer company's [premises] with a giant [shopping] mall – the Brewery. This was progress (*Max Bontoft*); 'I hope they keep building nice places for people to live in and be happy' (*Hannah Mehmet*); 'There is so much history in our town that it makes me proud to live in Romford. . . . To me Romford is a place where I meet my friends' (*Dane Curle*); 'It can be a good place to start a business or get a decent job' (*Raphael pupil*); 'A lot of people have jobs in Romford and a lot of other people use the train station like I do, and a lot of people live far from Romford but have to go there every day' (*Jason Wan*); 'Romford is such an enormous place it's easy to get lost in' (*Pryanka Vicchi*); 'To me Romford is like a mini-town, city and countryside in one; it is a really nice place . . . there is a lot more greenery than in London' (*Temitope Oshin*); 'Romford market is well known and attracts lots of people from outside the area. I am fond of Romford and although it doesn't have the best reputation it still feels like home to me' (*Joe Jacovou*); 'Romford is like a smaller version of London; it has a shop to suit everyone's needs. It also has a few good nightclubs for the teenager' (*Shianne Stannard*); 'Shopping malls and leisure will always be important, but they don't make us remember the true meaning of life and living in Romford. Romford is a place of leisure, sport, history and [has] a heart of gold' (*Oghosa Ovienrioba*); 'Romford will keep on growing into a modern sophisticated, new and enjoyable town to work and live in. A huge ice cream sundae!' (*Grace Quah*); 'The town is definitely growing and there are more places to spend time in with friends and family. It still has some nice parks such as Raphael Park. There are a good variety of churches and places of interest. There will be more people living here, so more schools will need to be built' (*Dannielle Henderson*).

And in conclusion: 'Romford is a very nice place to live – why don't you go and see for yourself?' (*James Broadbent*).

A spectacular view from above of Romford's busy Market Place when traffic still used the through route down the middle, 1959. On the top left can be seen the Duke of Wellington public house, and at right the extensive bulk of the King's Head, with its archway leading to the King's Hall at the back, once an important meeting place. Below the camera, underneath the church tower, from which the photograph was taken, is a Green Line coach on its way to Brentwood (once a service every 15 minutes). Beyond that the Eastern National double-decker from Southend advertises the Kursaal entertainment centre. Over the top of the King's Head can be seen the two bowling greens that lay behind the market properties.

Laurie Square Gardens were often a quiet oasis sheltered from the market by the Laurie Hall, and laid with flower beds. There is even a small topiary garden in front of the photographer, who is standing outside the group of Victorian townhouses at the back of the square. As can be seen, the square was the original site of the War Memorial, which was moved up to Coronation Gardens, Main Road, when the new ring road was constructed.

A 1950s view of the High Street, seen from the Golden Lion corner, reveals the old building on the left from which the *Romford Times* was published by the printers and stationers Wilson & Whitworth. This building, with which a number of ghost stories are associated, was later demolished to allow a wider footpath at this point.

Inset: The last days of the narrow High Street, summer 1966. The frontages were moved back and a wide pavement for pedestrians was created.

A view of the King's Head, *c.* 1966. It is flanked by Thompson's the fishmongers on the left at 32 Market Place and Liberty Pharmacies, which have modernised the lower part of their premises at no. 28. The King's Head survived for a few years before being demolished and being recreated in the new Mercury Gardens beside Mercury House. Later becoming a nightclub, this establishment no longer exists.

The Duke of Wellington just before demolition, 9 February 1967. The ubiquitous headscarf, very common up to this time, is worn by two ladies in front of the plant stall.

Left: A huge crowd gathered in 1969 to join the excitement of the market through-road closure, bringing to an end centuries of tradition. Bill Fuller, Mace Bearer, clears the way for the Mayor, Alderman Bill Smith and the Mayoress of Havering. The office of alderman was soon to be abolished. A certain amount of relief from motor traffic was now given to the centre of the town, with the opening of the northern part of the ring road. It would be some years before the circuit round the outside of the town centre was completed.

Inset: A procession at the back of the Market Place defines the more colourful period of the 1960 and '70s. The group, mostly connected with local drama societies and rigged out in Victorian dress, includes in the middle foreground Gordon Humby, librarian of Romford and of the new London borough created in 1965. The event was part of the celebrations for the closing of the old road through the market.

Above: As the 1950s gave way to the 1960s a new youth culture appeared in Romford as elsewhere, although this is not immediately apparent from this view of Church House. But look at the poster advertising events to be held in the hall, and you will see the Big Three, who had a hit with 'Some Other Guy' in 1963 and, on the same programme, the Roofraisers were due to appear at the Wykeham Hall. Another sign of the times was the coming of coffee bars, with their hissing Gaggia machines, a new gathering place for the youth of the town. The Beatles were in Romford at the Odeon as a supporting act. David Bowie brought the Aladdin Sane tour to the town in 1973, causing a huge queue for tickets, and Paul Simon performed a solo at Romford Folk Club in a room above the King's Head in the mid-1960s.

Above, right: The girls in the Rolls-Royce are from Gamages during its brief sojourn in the town. They are flanked by a 'B' type General bus, similar to some that once ran from Bow Road to Gidea Park, on the first motor bus route into the town, and by a vintage fire engine. As the 1970s progressed this kind of colourful spectacle became more common.

Right: Another 1970s event found Jimmy Savile hosting a 'Welcome to Citizenship' event at Romford library. He is seen here taking a rest in the company of five young library workers, in the Borough Librarian's office. Most of the young ladies are fashionably dressed in mini skirts, and two are wearing the high boots popular at the time. On other occasions the library staff organised a rock band concert and also performed songs and instrumental numbers from the days of love and peace. These were the days when hippies filled the streets of the town wearing caftans and long coats and sporting tinted shades. Exotic perfumes mingled with the smell of joss sticks. At least two underground magazines compiled in Romford were available on the streets, along with national titles such as *Oz*.

Previous page: After the heady days of hippydom, and even perhaps for those youngsters who did not dig the culture, Romford was thought rather a desert, lacking nightclubs and entertainment facilities, unlike today. One local paper ran the headline 'The town that dies at night', claiming 'many young people from all over Havering have deserted their home town in search of excitement. They find it anywhere, it seems, but Romford. But not everyone was unhappy. Public house managers, like those running the Cooper's Arms and the King's Head, are delighted that their pubs are the only young places for miles around.' The picture above shows an evening scene outside the Dolphin Leisure Centre, which was opened by the Duke of Gloucester on 14 April 1982. During its relatively short life it suffered a disastrous fire in the Banqueting Hall, caused by suspected vandalism, in January 1992 in spite of in-house CCTV coverage, and also temporary closure of the pool in 1993. With council cuts caused by local government cash crises, it was scheduled to close on 31 March 1995. In the earlier good days the building was an attractive venue, as a family leisure pool (it was not designed to cater for serious swimmers) and also for antique fairs, wedding fairs, dinners, dances and aerobics classes. But the design was not economic in the latter days of local government financial stringency.

North House, captured from the most flattering angle, dominates the Opium nightclub and other businesses in the pedestrianised section of North Street.

The Romford brewery yard, 1969. Large amounts of money had been invested in modern facilities. But yet more extensive alterations were to be carried out in 1980. Multinationals are a law unto themselves however, and all this infrastructure was trashed and the workers laid off when the brewery closed down in the 1990s.

Construction cranes loom over the rooftops of South Street in recent years. Romford is again being remodelled drastically with the new Brewery Centre rising gradually from the cleared site of Ind Coope's extensive brewery.

South Street today has been largely pedestrianised and banks and building societies occupy many of the buildings in the top half. This view from the Golden Lion displays an almost continental look. There is now a festive feel and a holiday atmosphere replacing the old workaday scene.

10

Part of the Community

The Rotary Club of Romford has now been part of the community for 82 years. As Peter Owen put it in an article celebrating the club's 75th anniversary in 1997, 'the British Broadcasting Company had just gone on air with its first regular news bulletin; Bonar Law's Tories were revelling, Blair-like, in their first days of power, having ousted Lloyd George. Mussolini swept in to seize control of Italy, and the final chapter of the infamous Bywaters murder was written as death sentences were passed on the two lovers from Ilford. Two days later, on December 13 1922, 8 miles away at Romford, history of another kind was being written, with the chartering of the Rotary Club of Romford, only the 78th to be formed in this country.' In fact the first step was recorded in a local newspaper on 15 February 1922, 'on Friday afternoon a number of prominent gentlemen met at the White Hart hotel at the invitation of Mr E.N. Wimhurst, a member of the London Rotary Club, to carry out the preliminaries of forming a club at Romford. . . . Mr Vivian Carter, General Secretary of the British Association of Rotary Clubs, explained the objects for which the Rotary movement stood, and explained the motto "Service above Self" . . . which would afford a Rotarian an opportunity to serve society. Mr Wimhurst then moved two resolutions: – That a Rotary Club be formed in Romford, under the auspices and in affiliation with the British Association, and that a provisional committee be formed to make the necessary preliminary arrangements and to report in a month's time.'

For the rest of 1922 a number of meetings were held with speakers on interesting subjects. The early members formed a provisional committee. They were: Reverend Charles Steer MC (Provisional Chairman and later First President of the Club), A.W. Gay LL.B, Solicitor (Provisional Hon. Secretary), A.H. Symons, Solicitor (Associate Member), Dr V.I. Levy, Physician, T. England JP, Pharmacist, A. Norris, Dentist, F. Hobday, Estate Agent, F. Gay, Surveyor and Auctioneer, A.H.M. Poole, Baker and Confectioner, H. Bristow, Postmaster, W. King, London Rotary Club and E.N. Wimhurst, London Rotary Club.

A lively meeting was held on 18 November 1922 at which nearly 40 members were present. A paper was given on 'The Case for Prohibition' by F.E. Potter, followed by 'The Case against Prohibition' by a member of the Anti-Prohibition League. Prohibition of alcohol, of course, became law in the USA for a time. At Romford there was 'a brief but spirited discussion'. Even this was not the end of the meeting, for Dr Levy spoke briefly on the Rotary Movement – Rotarians had plenty of stamina in 1922!

And so the club received its charter at a time when Romford and Britain were feeling the debilitating effects of the aftermath of the First World War. There was plenty of scope for service in the community. The town was also on the verge of other big changes that were to turn it from a sleepy country town into a prosperous regional centre. Several of its founding members were crucial catalysts of this change. Club members working together between the wars were able to create systems of self-help in the town, some of which anticipated features of the welfare state of the later decades of the century.

An important figure in the town in the 1920s was a member of the club. Thomas (Tommy) England saw with a great vision the future shape of the town, and its housing, recreational and charitable aspirations, which also took into account the importance of the younger generation. The latter is a key element in the workings of the modern club. Tommy purchased areas of land from the time he came to Romford as a young man, and was not only responsible for the development of areas such as Rise Park with a housing scheme, but also the adjacent open space. His big idea, in the words of Glyn Richards, 'was that it ought to be possible to walk from Romford on public land or land that could be acquired, all the way to Stapleford Abbots, and he proved the point on one occasion by inviting fellow Rotarian Philip Dales, an architect, and one other person . . . to walk from Romford station along Eastern Road, up through Lodge Farm, crossing the main road at Black's Bridge, passing through Raphael Park and on to what afterwards became known as Rise Park Boulevard, which England later helped to develop. He gave land on the other side of the arterial road (Eastern Avenue) to create Rise Park, and therefore there was a pathway going right through to Lower Bedfords Road, one crossed there, emerging from Bedfords Park near Fernside, then entering the Pyrgo Park estate, a footpath which emerged at Stapleford Abbots. Few people believed that his idea would come to fruition but in fact it did.' England was anticipating today's Thames Chase project. He was the second President of Romford Rotary Club and also Chairman of the Urban District Council in the early 1920s. But he was also involved in many other organisations such as the YMCA, which was founded in North Street and later moved to the Lambourne Hall in Western Road, which he helped to purchase. We also have England to thank for his part in securing the present substantial building at Roneo Corner.

In a delightfully headed newspaper article 'Croakers – Clear Out', reprinted from his address to the Rotary Club, he talked about the scheme for a community centre for Romford, as a kind of First World War memorial, which would do more for the town than a monument. The club was established in the grounds of the old vicarage in North Street. The hut was loaned by the YMCA and had been used at the Hare Hall Camp in the First World War. From this grew facilities to fulfil the stated aims: 'some place where citizens can rub shoulder to shoulder, exchange views, continue their education, and seek recreation'. Rotarians helped to refurbish the hut, aided by boys from Mawney Road School, where Rotarian Maskelyne was headmaster. All these activities having been got off the ground together with tennis courts, later became the YMCA. Remember this was a time for much commercial distress and unemployment, owing to the destruction of prosperity by the First World War and its after-effects.

Romford Rotary Club sponsored a number of organisations from this time on, often getting local people to carry on the cause after the associations had been set up. What was being provided was a measure of self-help. Today Rotary is an international organisation and has exported this idea to other countries where aid is required, seeding schemes with start-up funds to enable people in need to help themselves. Addressing the problems of the 1920s and '30s with the same kind of impetus, the club set up bodies like the Romford and Hornchurch Tuberculosis After-care Association. This disease was a terrible scourge among the poor because of inadequate food and bad diets.

It was in 1924 that, in the words of Glyn Richards, 'Dr Alfred Ball, the local Medical Officer of Health, urged the club to try and provide facilities for patients who had been discharged from sanatoria to obtain refreshing foods to recover their physical health. The Rotary Club worked with a will to get this association established, and the association . . . did a tremendous amount to help people get better.' Following up on this, individual Rotarians volunteered their services and the club gave funds to enable sick children recently returned from hospital to spend a week or two at Frinton or Clacton. Rotarians transported scores of children who were restored to full health. One Rotarian recalled that he took youngsters to Frinton. One boy lay on the back seat of the car, lacking the energy even to smile. He was so weak that it was deemed necessary to leave him at Frinton for three weeks, and the club received reports on his progress. Then the Rotarian who had taken him to Frinton went to bring him home again. The club was amazed to hear his report: 'I've never seen such a transformation. Poor little kid, when I took him there he seemed more dead than alive. When I brought him back yesterday he was more like a rampaging lion. I couldn't keep him still in the back of the car – he was all over it.'

One of the most important schemes in the interwar period was the founding in 1930 of the Romford Social Service Association. In Romford and Hornchurch in the later 1920s and early '30s there were thousands of local people queuing up at the dole office to receive their 30 shillings a week. A decline in international trade had seriously affected Britain and lowered the value of the currency. Local communities were not in theory depressed areas like Durham and the Welsh mining areas, but labour exchanges were the scene of long queues of the unemployed. The streets were filled with those who could do nothing day after day but wander aimlessly. Compared to today many were incredibly thin, had little to eat and nowhere to go. The Revd Philip Abraham, vicar of St Edward's in the Market Place, talked to the club about this problem: 'We must do something about it – you and I. We have to be good neighbours.'

The result was a small committee that worked fast in the name of the club to call a general meeting at the Wykeham Hall. This decided to set up the Romford Social Service Association, mobilising people in the town to deal with the problems. In the old building at the end of the Market Place, the Courthouse or old Town Hall, a soup kitchen was established. The demand was so enormous that soup was carried to the hungry by the Rotarians' wives and other ladies who were willing to help. Rotarians too peeled potatoes and prepared vegetables for cooking in the huge pots. More help was needed and a boxing and recreational club for boys began, and a sports club for girls. Rehabilitation groups were begun by Rotarians to get people back into a state where they could be employed. In addition a garment centre opened with appeals for discarded clothing that could be cleaned, repaired and distributed.

Another initiative was to establish a personal advice service. Rotarians' wives and friends gave what advice and assistance they could. This eventually became the Citizens Advice Bureau, which to this day is a valuable centre giving an excellent service to the town. Many other community projects were given a kick start by Rotarians in the interwar period, including ventures for the welfare of senior citizens. The Romford version was called the Veterans' Club, and was based at the Red Triangle Club in North Street.

When the Second World War came the club continued to serve in difficult conditions, maintaining its commitment to the Rotary ideal. Obviously a number of Rotarians were involved in national service, but still found time for Rotary commitments. The club joined up with Romford United Charities, for instance, to hold a Christmas party for pensioners in the Wykeham Hall in 1941. Nearly 300 people turned up for an afternoon of food, cups of tea, dancing and socialising. In 1943 the club established a hostel for servicemen passing through the town, for whom it was difficult to make other provision and who often had to sleep rough. In its first year it provided a night's accommodation for nearly 2,000 servicemen. A Rotary spokesman said at a meeting: 'since the hostel was opened the number of beds being added to it kept increasing. It has been in demand and attracted a lot of soldiers. When it first started there was some doubt as to its efficiency, as some men were using the brewery air raid shelter. But the . . . accommodation difficulty was accentuated by the number of American soldiers. The Red Cross will now be able to provide quarters for them, which will ensure that there are sufficient places for British troops at the hostel.' In March 1944, a new servicemen's hostel was opened in the old hall of the United Services Club in Romford High Street. This had 54 beds and could accommodate almost 20,000 soldiers a year. Money raised by the Rotary Club of Romford enabled the building to be completely redecorated. It was hoped that servicemen stranded overnight would be able to use the centre and get their own bunk, rather than use a public air raid shelter.

Since the war a great number of projects have been instituted by our parent organisation, Rotary International, whose 100th birthday was on 23 February 2005. Each year Rotarians contribute as part of their subscription a dedicated amount for the Rotary charity fund known as Foundation. This is part of Rotary's careful housekeeping. Funds raised from a club like Romford, for instance for clean water wells for a Ghanaian village, can be doubled from the Foundation fund if a properly submitted application is approved by the Trustees. Romford Rotary have recently supported many projects in this way, such as college materials (books and computers) for a school in the Lebanon. In connection with the Chernobyl Lifeline we have helped a clinic in Minsk, where children are still feeling the effects of the nuclear fallout from the catastrophic meltdown. We have also been able to copy another initiative by sending to children in Belarus shoeboxes filled with small Christmas presents. In many projects we have been able to join with our continental contact clubs, Dendermonde (Belgium) and Bruay (France), so that three sums of money build up to a grand total for one particular charitable cause. This tripartite friendship helps to cement relationships between countries: each has its own connections with parts of the developing world, facilitating a special Rotary aim as expressed at meetings: 'Rotary and Peace the World Over.' In the 1990s Rotarian Bob Vivers was honoured to serve as District Governor for our District 1240, which covers Havering, Essex, and the Stortford area of Hertfordshire. Several other members have also served at District level.

Locally we have raised funds for numerous projects, such as the St Francis Hospice, Samaritans, Hacton School unit for deaf children, Women's Refuge, providing fold-up beds for parents staying at Harold Wood Hospital when their child is ill, and in our 75th year, a vital signs monitor for Oldchurch Hospital Children's Ward. Each year we arrange a Borough 'Youth Speaks' competition, mock interviews for school pupils, and our own music competition. In order to raise funds we hold a social event such as an evening at the Greyhound Stadium, and funds from this will not only help Havering Hospice but contribute to presenting over 1,000 copies of this book to Year 7 pupils at Romford schools. We are pleased that the book includes not only contributions/memories from older residents, but also from children at local schools. This account has necessarily only skimmed the surface of a great sea of initiatives undertaken by the club over the years, and continued year by year up to the present time, but as Rotary progresses into the new millennium we hope to renew our membership with local business and professional people, and others wanting to help, men and women, who are invited to visit what we believe is the friendliest organisation in Havering – the Rotary Club of Romford.

Romford Library was based in the old Charity School building at the top end of the Market Place in 1930, after a long struggle by the Rotary Club to persuade the local authorities that it was a vital element of a civilised town.

Caricatures by Matt show three local Rotarians and their other roles in Romford in 1932. Councillor C.H. Allen became charter mayor when Romford became a borough in 1937.

The Marshalls Park team, the most recent of our winners in the 'Youth Speaks' competition, went on to capture the District Final at Chelmsford's County Hall. They are seen with the Mayor of Brentford.

Opposite, above: A magic evening, one of many social events arranged by the club.

Opposite, below: Romford Rotary Club contributed funds towards 'Bookstart', a national scheme to encourage very young children to get acquainted with books and reading. This is the scene at a launch event at Harold Hill Library.

The trio from Campion School who progressed from the Romford competition to win the same event the previous year.

An incredible array of musical talent at the 2004 Music Competition. Our winner, holding the 75th anniversary cup, went on to represent Romford at the District Final.

Our friends from Bruay and Dendermonde joined us to celebrate our 75th anniversary in 1997.

The banners of our contact clubs on the continent.

Contributors

MARSHALLS PARK SCHOOL

Sam Brown
Samantha Curran
Jessica Day
Jason Frost
Kathryn Grant
Alfie Harper
Courtney Harrison
Stephanie Jarman
James Jefferson
Andrew Jones
Jennifer Jones
John Kelly
Shanta Lall
Andrew Lewis

James Long
Sandy Ortanca
Abbie Payne
Alex Phillips
Chelsea Putnam
Luke Redpath
Kieran Richardson
Sarah Russell
Tina Tayeby
Luke Tisser
Alice Warren
David Waters
Dean Williams
David Wilson

RAPHAEL SCHOOL

Stephanie Aldis
Max Bontoft
James Broadbent
Dane Curle
Mathew Esan
Jasdev Hothi
Dannielle Henderson
Joe Jacovou
Hannah Mehmet

Daniel Ong
Temitope Oshin
Oghosa Ovienrioba
Amy Porter
Grace Quah
Shianne Stannard
Levi Thornton
Priyanka Vichhi
Jason Wan

SENIOR CONTRIBUTORS

J. Arnold
D.W. Clark
B. Collett
P.A. Corbell
E. Fisk

A. Gilbert
R.E. Giles
J. Hewitt
J. Kirk
K. Langridge

B. Matthews
P. Owen
L. Poole
G. Richards
A. Rudkins

B. Smith
D.H. Starr
A.E. Thompson
C. Vale

Acknowledgements

All pictures are the property of the author, apart from those listed here.

D. Bond	p. 126 (both)	D. Paton	p. 76
P. Cooper	p. 98 (top)	R. Prince	title page
J. Copeland	pp. 5, 20, 38 (top), 44 (top), 46 (top), 79, 95 (bottom), 96 (top)	B. Rider	pp. 45 (top), 50–1, 94 (bottom)
K. Godfrey	p. 78	B. Smith	pp. 30 (bottom), 40 (drawing)
K. Langridge	pp. 45 (bottom), 57 (bottom), 88	R. Squire	pp. 106–7, 110–11
		P. Steer	pp. 102, 112 (top)
Mrs B. Nelson	pp. 98–9	C. Vale	p. 95 (top)